Make 'Em Beg to Work for You!

7 Steps to Find, Hire, Manage, Reward, and Release All-Star Players to Help Make Your Dream a Reality

DR. ANGELA E. LAURIA

DIFFERENCE PRESS

Difference Press

Washington, D.C., USA

Copyright © Angela Lauria, 2019

Difference Press is a trademark of Becoming Journey, LLC

All rights reserved. No part of this book may be reproduced in any form without permission in writing from the author. Reviewers may quote brief passages in reviews.

Published 2019

ISBN: 978-1-68815-228-1

DISCLAIMER No part of this publication may be reproduced or transmitted in any form or by any means, mechanical or electronic, including photocopying or recording, or by any information storage and retrieval system, or transmitted by email without permission in writing from the author. Neither the author nor the publisher assumes any responsibility for errors, omissions, or contrary interpretations of the subject matter herein. Any perceived slight of any individual or organization is purely unintentional. Brand and product names are trademarks or registered trademarks of their respective owners.

Art Direction: Michelle Grierson

Editor: Grace Kerina

Author's photo courtesy of Jenn Reid

For Rae

Thank you for pushing me out of my comfort zone in all the best ways.

TABLE OF CONTENTS

CHAPTER 1
Why Won't People Just Do What I Tell Them?   1

CHAPTER 2
A Million Dreams   15

    Aspie and Proud. 18

    Logo Matters. 23

    Side Note 27

CHAPTER 3
Ending Dick-Centric Business-Building Tactics   29

    Communication is Impossible 31

    Why Can't I Pay People to Do What I Want Them to Do? 33

    Treat Your Team Even Better than Your Clients 37

    Rockstar Employees Don't All Look and Think Like You 40

CHAPTER 4
Not a Moment. A Movement   43

    Alignment Requires Clarity. 45

    Your Dream Team 49

    What OTHER Problem Does Working for You Solve? 53

    Step 1 Conclusion: Cultivate Controversy 56

CHAPTER 5
There Is No Bus (#sorrynotsorry)   57

You Can't Clone Yourself. That's Not a Thing. 59

Tedious, But Powerful Task List 61

Find the Gaps 64

Focus Everyone on Their Strengths 65

Step 2 Conclusion: Operate into the Future 68

CHAPTER 6
If You Only Read One Chapter, Make It This One   71

The Philosophy Behind the Approach .74

What Is Your Ideal Candidate's Problem and Dream Come True?.77

Part 1: The Title Is Not the Title. 80

   Write the title for the first position you are going to fill. 82

Part 2: Problem and Dream Come True 82

      Managing Editor 83

      Junior Editor/Editorial Intern 85

      IT Specialist. 85

Part 3: Responsibilities with a Twist 86

Part 4: Process to Apply 90

Part 5: Who We Are / Our Values 93

Step 3 Conclusion: Market to Your Prospective Workers 97

CHAPTER 7
You Had Me at Hello   99

The Screening Begins 101

The Written Project 104

The Interview 107

Closing the Deal & Salary Negotiation 110

Step 4 Conclusion: Pick the winners 113

CHAPTER 8
Incubating Intrinsic Motivation   117

Salary Bands 120

Performance Bonuses 123

Commissions 129

High-Potential Employees (HiPots) 130

Structuring Raises 132

Benefits. 137

Step 5 Conclusion: Align the Compensation 139

CHAPTER 9
Slow Is Smooth. Smooth Is Fast   141

Hire Before You Need 'Em 143

The First 90 Days 146

Less Than You Think, But Better 150

Step 6 Conclusion: Nurture the Talent. 155

CHAPTER 10
Letting Go   157

An Object in Motion. 159

No Sudden Moves 161

The Difference Between Nurturing and Dragging It Out 165

Step 7 Conclusion: Yield with Love 170

CHAPTER 11
The Prize Never Chases — 173

CHAPTER 12
The Multi-Orgasmic Business — 189

- There's No I in COMPANY 193
- Step 1: Culture First 194
- Step 2: Operate in the Future 194
- Step 3: Market to Your Prospective Workers 194
- Step 4: Pick the winners 195
- Step 5: Align the compensation 196
- Step 6: Nurture your Talent 197
- Step 7: Yield with Love 197

Acknowledgments — 201
About the Author — 209
About Difference Press — 212
Other Books by Dr. Angela Lauria — 215
Other Books by Difference Press — 216
Thanks for Reading — 218

CHAPTER 1

Why Won't People Just Do What I Tell Them?

Kate and Grace sat me down after only a few months on my team. Both experienced and talented editors, they were finding themselves overwhelmed by details and logistics and, frankly, things just changed too quickly for the job to feel like fun. There were always special exceptions and extensions and delays. It was hard to plan their own lives and taking a vacation was impossible. The job was 24/7/365 and while the compensation I offered was good for most editing roles, it wasn't enough to make it worth the insanity of a job with a startup that never seemed to stop changing.

It was hard to hear their complaints. As 2 of my first employees, paying them was so hard. Mostly their monthly fees went on my credit card and I hoped someday the business would work. The answers to all their complaints sounded expensive and as I was still losing money on every new client I couldn't figure out how to address their problems without going broke in the process.

Why wouldn't they just take a risk and believe in me?

If they just worked as hard as I did I would reward them for sticking with me. Someday the company would be making millions and they would have senior roles and share in the profits.

What did I have to do to get them to see they were much better off working hard for me now than setting these ridiculous boundaries?

I called a friend. Threw a tantrum. Waved my fists in the air. And then carefully crafted a response. "I've heard your feedback and I think you are right. I can't fix it all right now but we can start. I'm going to hire you an assistant to help with the administrative tasks and cover for you if you need to take a vacation."

It wasn't much, but it was enough to buy time.

I knew I needed a better plan. But what?

Maybe lower-wage workers in remote locations and more of them?

Or people who needed the jobs more?

What to do was not clear to me at all but what was clear was that it felt like editing these books myself would take less time than hiring and managing other people to do it. Now I was going to spend as much time managing these 2 editors and the assistant as I was editing the books myself, and they were all going to be unhappy about it as I went broke.

This is when the fantasies about moving to Hoi An (an adorable and cheap town with a great expat community in Vietnam) started. I would take 4 clients a year at $100K each and live like a queen in Vietnam or Thailand. When I wasn't trying to manage my small but growing staff, I was dreaming about my great escape. The burden of building a team felt impossible.

I had a designer at the time. Talented guy. But the story there was the same. The covers were late. The interiors were full of dumb mistakes. And the reason for all of that was always me. Too many special situations. Too many changing deadlines. Too much last-minute.

It was frustrating because those deals they were complaining about – they were the only ones paying the bills. If they thought it was so easy not to have special cases and changing deadlines, why didn't they make the sales?

I hired. I fired. I watched great people quit. I tried different tactics. Read all the books. Even went to Florida for a consultation with my father.

My dad, Mickey Lauria, is in the Hot Rod Hall of Fame. My dad was in the Hot Rod business for almost 40 years. At its peak, Total Performance, my dad's company, had 22 employees, 8,000 square feet, and $5M in revenue. He is retired now and I really wanted him to look at what I was doing in my business and drop some serious knowledge bombs on me to get me out of this employee spin cycle.

"Middle management," said my dad over a Starbucks Latte. "That's what I did wrong. I didn't invest enough in middle management. Oh, and meetings. You need more meetings and more middle management. Yup. That is the answer. Middle management?"

I left Florida and headed north absolutely scratching my head. Middle management? What did that even mean? Pay people to manage other people doing the work? Where was this money coming from? And had my father's mental health started to decline? How on God's earth could this be the answer?

When I was growing up, we talked about my dad's business at every family meal. Inevitably, he would tell my mom a story of another stupid employee doing another stupid thing.

"So I looked him in the eye," he'd tell my mom, "and I said, 'I don't pay you to think!'"

It wasn't the first time I'd heard that phrase. In fact, "I don't pay you to think" was my dad's mantra. He was in a permanent state of frustration caused by his employees.

My dad was the kind of guy you whispered about if you worked for him or with him. He can eviscerate someone with the slightest turn of phrase. As much as my dad hated his employees, his employees seemed to hate him. And yet many of them would beg for their jobs back after quitting in disgust just months prior. As much as they hated him, they were draw to his passion and vision.

About 4 years into my journey with The Author Incubator, I was struggling with hiring and managing employees. I had the passion and the vision, but people were not loving working for me. I assumed this was because, like my dad, I was a difficult person to work for. I wanted to know why his employees came back even though he had a sharp tongue and didn't particularly pay well, so I reached out to some of those employees who'd begged for their jobs back and asked why.

This message from one of those employees was the single most critical moment in my journey growing The Author Incubator:

"Your dad wasn't the easiest man to work for, but it was only because he expected perfection in every department, after many talks in his office I started to see my faults, I was very proud of the potential he saw in me, it made me see how important everything I did in there was.

"He came to me one day, we had a toilet changed out in a bathroom, the new one was smaller than the old one... I got some paint, without asking and painted the wall so it would match, then I cleaned the whole thing... he pulls me aside and asked if I did that? Nervous I said yes, sorry I should have asked, he said that's the kinda thing you gets you a raise!! He said the phrase (that's not my job doesn't apply, if everyone had your view on this place, I'd be a much happier man.... he said Rivers, you're doing great, keep it up...."

Bill Rivers, the guy who sent me this message, ended it by saying, "I wouldn't have traded my time there for anything, I definitely would not be who I am had it not been for him...," and that, I realized, was the missing link. I had to CREATE opportunities that would make this sentiment "I wouldn't trade my time there for anything" inevitable.

My dad always said, "I don't pay you to think." But the truth is, it's all he ever wanted from his employees, he just didn't want to say it because he was afraid of people disappointing him.

If I was going to outpace my dad's success, I had to become willing to be disappointed.

I realized the reason Bill worked so hard for my dad was that he didn't see himself as an employee, as much as he saw himself as a student.

"It was very beneficial for me to have learned so much from him," he said.

Funny, because I wasn't thinking about how the jobs I was giving my employees were beneficial to them beyond a paycheck, and yet Bill didn't mention money once.

With my employees, I would hire anyone qualified and willing to take my money in exchange for their time. But that's not what Bill Rivers was doing with my dad. Bill was excited to share his time with my dad because "he was surely a great role model for me growing up, after all I was 18 when I first started there, couldn't even concave how intelligent he was."

The value of the job was much more than the paycheck.

I began to only hire candidates who could enunciate to me what – other than money – they needed from the job.

I began to apply the same rules of client selection to my hiring process. In my business I help people write, publish, and promote non-fiction books that add an extra $250K - $500K a year to their businesses. But if I have a candidate who wants to write fiction, or doesn't want to do marketing,

I won't accept them into the program because I will not take money from someone who is struggling with a problem I don't help people solve.

As an employer I needed to apply the same exact principle and begin to understand the PROBLEM the job was going to solve in my prospective employee's life.

Once I had a team for whom their job was solving a problem much bigger than paying their bills, it became possible to take a giant step backwards from the business.

A couple months after reading this message, and a year after my dad suggested the missing link was meeting and middle management, I told my team, "I pay you to think. I want you guys to care about this place more than I do."

And I'm willing to be disappointed in ways my dad wasn't, because I know that willingness is required for us to go where we are going.

In order to outpace my dad, I had to pay people to think. I'm proud to say I've been able to hire people who are BETTER at what they do than I am and every day it gets easier and more fun to pay them to think.

Most businesses I observe are like my dad's. They don't pay people to think. There might have been a time in history where that worked, but with a largely millennial workforce now, that approach will not fly. Millennials will not just work for money, and, by the way, why would you want a staff member who was only in it for the money? When the job you can offer is the solution to a problem money can't solve, you will have an employee who will work smarter and harder on one aspect of your business than you ever could with all you have to deal with as a business owner.

The truth is, you don't want someone on your team who doesn't want to be there. You want a team filled with people who could have their pick of any job in the world and they pick working for you and your company.

I didn't think that was possible for me for a long time. I had to change my thoughts about money, about millennials and meetings, and about middle management before I could really see the power of building a world-class team.

The single most significant thing I've done in my journey with The Author Incubator, and possibly in my whole life, is learn how to build a highly functional team. The reason that I know we will hit $100 Million in the next 5 years is precisely because I learned how to pay people to think. I'm righting my dad's wrongs so that I can enjoy the benefits of all my "rights." That email from Bill Rivers, one of my dad's most loyal employees, was the inspiration for my commitment to build a team. I hope this book inspires you to do the same. Employees deserve more awesome places to work and the difference you will be able to create with your business is exponential when you have a team on your side.

Before we get started you should know the reasons it will be hard for you will be different than the reasons it was hard for me. But make no mistake, building an organization that has prospective employees begging to work for you will be one of the hardest things you ever do, but the rewards from your effort will blow you away.

CHAPTER 2

A Million Dreams

I was 9 or 10 and in a smallish town when I fell in love with Michael Jackson's music. I didn't know much about the world. Michael Jackson provided the background music. I listened to Thriller then as much as I listen to Hamilton now (and that's saying something).

Michael had 2 friends in the early 80s that captured my attention: Elizabeth Taylor and Ryan White. Ryan was a young hemophiliac, just a couple years older than me and he had AIDS but Michael loved him. If Michael wasn't afraid of Ryan I wasn't going to be either.

Elizabeth Taylor was passionate about supporting people with AIDS too, but she was always talking about gay men with AIDS. I learned that gay men were dying in epic proportions and the discrimination they faced made it harder to stop the spread of the disease or to find a cure. "Hey! What about my friend Ryan? Discrimination is hurting him too!"

And as that simple realization kicked in, I became a gay rights activist by the time I was 11 years old. In 6th grade I proudly wore my "Silence = Death" button with flair.

Years later when I was in my 20s and Michael Jackson's song "Man in the Mirror" came out, I'd listen to it on repeat in my Discman in my car. I would pull over to the side of the road on the George Washington Parkway. I'd stare across the Potomac at the monuments, listening to Michael declaring he was starting with the man in the mirror and asking him to change his ways to make the world a better place and I promised myself to "make that change," no matter what it took.

But it was on July 13, 1985 that I realized making a difference was going to require more than a passion for equality. I was 12 and I'd just watched the Live Aid benefit concert. I saw that starving girl in Ethiopia and I wanted to help.

Bob Geldof made me want to raise lots of money to help others. I know in retrospect those campaigns were imperfect. But they inspired me to get a team of middle school students together to wash cars on Route 5 in my little town in Wallingford, Connecticut. The summer of Live Aid we raised $1800 for the Prince's Trust Fund. And that was the summer I learned to organize and lead for change.

That was when I knew there was no way to make a difference in a high-impact, global way without making money.

I met Richard Branson, Virgin Group founder, entrepreneur, and philanthropist on Halloween of 2018 at his private game reserve in Ulusaba, South Africa. I was so excited to talk to him about money and business because we share a philosophy about the purpose of it all.

"I never went after the money," he told me. "If you can make a difference you gotta get out there and make a difference, I think. The advantage of being successful rather than not successful is you can do lots of good things with the money, like tackle some of the world's big problems."

What surprised me though, was Sir Richard's advice. No matter what the question was, his answer went back to building a team. Going all the way back to his earliest ventures with a music magazine, Richard always surrounded himself with implementers who, according to his own descriptions, stated multiple times, were better than him. He credits his dyslexia with giving him the foresight to realize he wasn't going to be able to do it on his own. He had the vision but needed a team.

Aspie and Proud

Most of my career had been focused on doing everything myself and intermittently paying people and being angry about their inability to complete tasks to my satisfaction. One of my bosses in the corporate world described my style as "very transactional" and it was. My thought was – I give you money, you do a task. It seemed like a reasonable trade. If I give you enough money you should be inspired to do the task well. Intuitively it never made any sense to me that that wouldn't work. It seemed like if you could get the compensation number right then you would always be able to get the task completed. To be honest, I still don't 100% understand why this doesn't work, but it 100% doesn't work.

Richard Branson always says being dyslexic was his biggest advantage. For me, having a form of high-functioning autism called Asperger's Syndrome has been my biggest advantage. I share this neuropsychology with Thomas Jefferson, Steve Jobs, Marie Curie, Albert Einstein, Shakespeare, Darwin, Picasso, Aristotle, and I'm sure a host of others known by a single name. Being Aspie allows me to focus on one object without becoming distracted and I can remember and process the most minute of details without getting lost or overwhelmed.

(It's so fun!) I make logical and rational decisions and stick to my course of action without being swayed by impulse or emotional reactions. I have never been a shiny object kind of entrepreneur. I set a goal, and I reach it.

I make the craziest connections between different disciplines other people simply can't see. My non-neurotypical nature makes it pretty much impossible for me to fall prey to social pressures or fears. I have no choice but to march loudly to the beat of my own drummer. I've always styled myself after Kassandra from Greek Mythology who was doomed to tell the truth and have no one believe her. My ability to recognize and speak the truth that everyone else is conveniently ignoring has been convenient for me – though not a feature enjoyed by my teachers or HR departments.

I am proud of being Aspie. But being Aspie comes with some downsides.

Asperger's is a developmental disorder characterized by significant difficulties in social interaction and nonverbal communication, along with restricted and repetitive patterns of behavior and interests. I have crippling Social Anxiety. (So crippling I felt the need to capitalize those letters for no good reason except it has capital letters inside my head.) My emotions are almost always misinterpreted by others and I horribly misinterpret others' emotions. I am unbearably sensitive to sounds, lights, smells, and touch. These are sensitivities that an individual who does not have Asperger's wouldn't notice.

The truth is, I am a fucking AMAZING human, but not a particularly likeable one. In The Author Incubator culture guide it says, "You are an ambassador of me, Angela Lauria: I am a mercurial, extremely opinionated, powerful, wildly brilliant, nurturing and generous person. I can be a hard person to represent. You may even find yourself having to explain or apologize for me. This may be challenging. Ask for help and guidance from people who have been here longer. For what it's worth, I have been diagnosed on the autism spectrum. I am also well aware that people have strong feelings about me. You don't have to hide that from me or try to convince people to like me. And you never have to lie. I have come to deep awareness and peace about who I am."

I would not be where I am without Asperger's and yet the limitations of this condition mean the very thing that came easiest to Richard Branson, building a team, is the thing I am least capable of in the world.

Like Sir Richard, I see it as my responsibility to be a steward for as much of the world's wealth as possible so I can use that money to protect and nurture the ways I see of healing the planet and the hearts of the people in it. I am here to make a difference and making a difference requires money. Full stop.

But money requires entrepreneurship. And entrepreneurship is throttled without the ability to build a team. Meeting Richard confirmed for me what I had come to realize with 5 years in business: to achieve my potential, I had to step completely out of the way. My Asperger's handicapped my ability to build a team, to get my business to the next level, so I needed leaders who could do things I can't – translate the systems we have built into tasks that can be reasonably executed.

Logo Matters

At Necker, Richard's private island in the Caribbean, he told me, "Find people who are better than you to do the day-to-day. Make sure they have the tools to do the job. Fix it quickly and invest more if they don't."

When you do that, you "make 'em beg" to work for you because they are working at a place with an incredible mission where they are heard, respected, and nurtured as employees. One of the things Richard told me was important for team building was the branding. He said I should have a logo my employees should want to get as a tattoo.

That's the formula!

This was hard for me because I have always recoiled against branding and focused instead on the results my clients got, with no pretty designs. When Richard said to think about branding as a way to attract and keep the best talent, I got interested.

I know without a team, I can't be successful.

I know that building a team is not a natural strength for me.

Left to my own devices I hired people who looked like me. People who thought like me. And people who had backgrounds and experiences like me.

On the one hand I was saying I wanted to make a difference – and for me, making a difference has always come down to expanding civil rights for people like me who don't fit into the middle-of-the-bell-curve model of being straight, white, cisgender, neurotypical humans. I care about the oppressed and the underserved because being non-neurotypical, differently bodied, queer, and female, I have always been able to see myself in the injustices of the world. I would be the first one shot in any revolution. I've wanted to create safe spaces for more voices to be heard since that first hustle at 12 years old.

And yet, my team was all like me. I wanted diversity in my clients, but I wasn't building it in my team. I just wanted to pay people who looked like me to do tasks without complaining and with efficiency. I know you might want that too going into this book. I get it. But I've got to tell you, it's not going to happen that way.

Making 'em beg to work for you is all about being a company, like the companies in the Virgin Group, that is WORTH begging to work for. You have to become the leader of a company people would beg to work for.

In this book you will find some super fun and creative tactics that will get you little wins here and there, but the true victory can only come if you implement the whole system. This won't matter if you want a little local business that makes your corner of the world or the Internet a better place. You can use these systems to hire one or two people a little more easily. But if we are working toward 90,000 people and $20 BILLION in revenue instead of $20 Million, which is where I am today with 45 employees, then you'll have to do much more than implement a few of the tricks here.

That said, in getting to a run-rate of $20M while managing my own Asperger's (often not well), I have learned a lot about what to do and what not to do in building a team. In this book, I'm going to share some of those hard-won lessons and also I'll try to decomplicate some of the massively complex, Aspie-infused systems I've created to hire an amazing staff that lets me step out of the way, so that you can apply them in your business.

As I write this from the deck at the Great House on Necker Island, entrepreneurs are facing one of the tightest labor markets in history. To get the best and the brightest to build your dreams alongside you, you have to separate yourself and your business so that others will want to dedicate a significant part of their life to helping you to shine. If building a team was easy for me, I probably wouldn't have had to learn these techniques, but perhaps because it's not something that comes easy to me, I have developed some systems I'm really proud of. I hope they help you to build your dream team too.

Side Note

In June of 2019, shortly after completing this manuscript and sharing this story with my team, one of my employees marched to the tattoo shop closest to our office and got our logo placed squarely on her shoulder blade. It was a humbling moment and a moment where I knew for sure, my business would outlive me.

CHAPTER 3

Ending Dick-Centric Business-Building Tactics

Let's get one thing straight before we start. I love men. I am the mother of a boy. I am not even 100% sure I would call myself a "feminist" – the term feels loaded to me – loaded with a bunch of crap I don't even believe.

What I do believe is that biologically men (in aggregate) are physically stronger than women and based on the animal kingdom's rules of dominance, through their physical strength, they became "king of the jungle." As the alphas of the species, the structures and institutions of society were created by men who had unconscious biases which influenced how those structures were created. I call the results of those unconscious biases in business – dick-centric tactics.

Please know my use of the clinical phrase dick-centric doesn't mean that I think men are assholes. It doesn't even mean that I think dick-centric tactics are dumb. It just means they are old structures based on a time when physical strength is what made you king of the jungle.

Physical strength is no longer the most important feature in deciding dominance and pecking order. Our society has transitioned from nomadic to farming and then to industry (areas where strength matters most) but beginning in 1970 or so, we have transition to the information age and soon I believe the experience age (areas where emotional strength matters most). The transition process we are in now is one of balancing out the dick-centric practices that were developed by patterning male biological systems to multi-orgasmic practices that pattern female biological systems. The final result of these swings will have a balancing effect or a more gender-neutral effect on society.

Right now, what is happening is that the dick-centric models from the pre-information age have Erectile Dysfunction. That's why these masculine systems are collapsing.

Incidentally, I believe the most emotionally strong genders are not bound by a traditional binary classification. The winners in the experience age will be gender non-binary folx, transgender people, and people who feel more gender fluid. But let's not get ahead of ourselves!

Communication is Impossible

I know what it's like to have a vision that you can't execute alone and to want people to do exactly what you tell them – or what you imagine you have told them – or, let's be honest, can't they just read your mind and do what you want them to do?

Communication is hard. Impossible even. And getting what you want does not come from hiring smart people and telling them what to do. Why not? EMOTIONS! This is how we know the end of the era of physical strength and dominance has come to a conclusion.

Old, male-based institutions are crumbling in the light of the unstoppable rise of the feminine. I'm going to get into Hegel's master/slave dialectic and some third-wave feminism in the following pages, but even if you ignore the philosophy bits explaining the phenomenon, you feel it, right? As a culture, we are no longer content with hierarchy. We aren't going to listen to our bosses or our elders mindlessly. This is the era of the whistleblower. (Thanks, Chelsea Manning!)

There is feminine inside all of us, no matter what gender (if any) resonates with us. When you have an intuitive hit – consciously or subconsciously – that something isn't right for you, you will find yourself not doing it. You might call this procrastination, or laziness, or disorganization – but what it really is, is the divine feminine inside of you, telling you this is not what you should be doing right now.

Structures in our society under the eras of physical dominance were based on your submission and compliance. This is how the patriarchy and white supremacy have thrived. But I know you can feel how those systems are collapsing. That's because the divine masculine (which is essential to life on the planet) has been out of balance. We need some more yin to go with our yang.

Why Can't I Pay People to Do What I Want Them to Do?

In the following pages I'll be talking about how the hyper fetishizing of the masculine has led to a lot of disappointment for small business owners. When you are just starting a business, it doesn't take long to realize, no matter how good you are at anything – or everything – you can't do it alone. If you are like me, you will want to pay people money and have them do it for you at least as well if not better than you could do it yourself.

You might have trouble finding people. You might find they are too expensive. Or you might have trouble managing them and getting the results you want. But either way, it won't be long before you realize that building and growing a team is not nearly as easy as it appeared to be from the outside.

This is because from the media and popular culture perspective, the patriarchy is still intact (barely). You put a hierarchy in place – even if it's a hierarchy of you and one other person, and what's supposed to happen is that everyone listens flawlessly and with no inner conflicts to the person above them in the hierarchy. In real life, it doesn't work this way, as you might have noticed. This is because yin and yang are moving back into balance. The pendulum is swinging back to center – and maybe even a little bit more strongly to the yin side – but the messages sent out to business owners have not caught up. This book is an attempt to bring that messaging into alignment with the actual state of reality.

This isn't a men and women thing at all – it's a masculine and feminine energy thing. MEN aren't the problem, but the patriarchy is an old system that no longer serves us (just like white supremacy, though I will address that less than I'd like in this book). Men get more benefits from patriarchal systems than women do as individuals – but as managers the patriarchy hurts men even more. Men will no longer be able to get their teams to listen to them and this will be even MORE confounding and challenging for them to remediate.

Having a clear list of tasks for an employee was the old way of doing things. This is what I mean when I say "masculine" or "dick-centric" when I'm being seemingly flippant. It's the idea that I am going to have a singular goal and keep thrusting away at it until I achieve satisfaction is a thing of the past. It can happen once in a while, but we are all transitioning together into the era of the multi-orgasmic business. It's no longer about set goal, break goal down into parts, hire people to bang away at each of the parts, reward for achievement, punish for failure. GOD! Those days were so simple and uncomplicated.

Now, we all are on the complex systems and multi-tasking train. As the business owner you are going to need to set a clear vision – but something bigger and more important, and more sustaining to the planet, than a revenue or profit target. More is required of you. To "make 'em beg" to work for you, you have to enroll people in a vision that goes way beyond your business itself and reaches to your community, your country, and maybe even the world.

Interestingly, the way you get people to beg to work for you is, in many ways, the way you get them to beg to be your client. You have to be awesome. A lot of leaders talk about building a brand, but I think all too often that gets translated into having a great designer who does a nice logo and making sure you use consistent fonts and colors. Let me tell you, employees (like clients) see RIGHT through that. Design will not save you. You have to know who you are and what you stand for. You have to live your personal life and your business in integrity with that vision. You need to treat your team exactly the way you treat your clients – probably better.

Treat Your Team Even Better than Your Clients

I used to think my clients were the ones I served. They were the important ones. And my team helped me serve them and in exchange I gave them money. Maybe even as you read those last two sentences you found yourself thinking, yeah, exactly, how else could it work? Well, I'm here with a news flash! Your team is your first and most important client. Yes, you OFFSET their payment to you of their TIME with some money – but as we all know, time is more valuable than money and it can't be replaced. Your team members are your most important clients and your job, first and foremost, is to serve them. If you don't do that – they will not serve your clients as well as you want them to.

The product you have "sold" your team is your vision. You have to sell each team member on the fact that you accomplishing your vision will help them to get something they want.

The way you get clients is that you convince them that implementing your vision will solve their problem. That is the exact same way you get a team that "begs" to work for you.

By the way, I am using the word "beg" here for a specific reason. It's a very emotionally evocative word. You may think people who have prospective clients or prospective employees begging to work with or for them have some magic something you don't have. Beyoncé can have people begging to work for her – but it's something that feels beyond most normal humans' grasp. What I want to show you in this book is that the reason people would give their right arm to work for Bey or Michelle Obama or Oprah is because it would be a win-win. It's not the person themselves that's magical, it's the payoff for your ego or your future that motivates people.

What "celebrity" employers have that you probably don't is an obvious forward-facing upside for anyone who comes to work for them. Sometimes we call this a "resume-builder," or people will say, "I'll do it for a couple years and then I can write my own ticket." Well, that is one kind of a win-win. The celebrity employer gets a dedicated staff member and the staff member gets more options and flexibility for their next gig.

This is a pretty basic and low-level win-win. You can do even better NOT being a celebrity. It can be technically easier to pass over the running of a non-celebrity company, since the business stands for itself then, instead of requiring the celebrity's involvement. The trick is you have to set a vision and dig your heels in about who you are even MORE firmly than a celebrity because you don't have the media helping you to amplify that vision. And, you are going to have to more closely listen to the needs and goals of your prospective employees.

Rockstar Employees Don't All Look and Think Like You

In this book I'm going to show you how to do just that. We will start with the vision for your company and your team. Once you have that we will build out the job descriptions in a fast and practical way as well as establishing the order in which you will be filling those roles. Once you are ready to start putting people onto the team, you will use the precise formula I use to write mind-blowing, rock star-attracting job descriptions based on tried and true techniques of direct response marketing, and then I'll show you how to use the interview process to make sure you make the right decision and how to compensate employees to get the best results – a lot of surprises in that chapter. Once you have the person hired, you still have a 50/50 chance of having someone who is a fit. It's a bummer, but the first 3 months are an incredibly vulnerable time and this person may not be a fit. I'll show you how to properly onboard someone to give them the best chance for success and if it doesn't work out I'll show you how to say goodbye with grace and ease.

Throughout this book we will be talking about areas where you might be unintentionally expressing bias regarding people's gender, race, physical differences, and their sexual partner gender preference. I am passionate about civil rights for all people. I am someone who has physical and mental differences. I have been over 200 pounds overweight and I have been diagnosed with Autism Spectrum Disorder. I am also queer and a woman. My own differences have made me particularly defensive about others' differences, but that's not why you will catch me on my soapbox in this book. What I have learned, because of my own sensitivities, is that people with different abilities and experiences have many traits that are desirable in staff members. That's not to say straight, white, cisgender folx don't have a lot to contribute too – they do – but as you will learn, it will always be easiest for you to find people most like you to hire. If you can fight against this natural, almost gravitational force, what you will find is a huge financial payoff (in addition to the moral and social payoffs).

By having a diverse team, you will open up minority markets in ways you might not have expected. I hear a lot of business owners saying they want people of color as clients, for instance, but I look at their staff and it doesn't look like a company that really "gets" the black, or, in the US, the African-American, experience. Essentially your staff telegraphs whether your company is a safe place for gay people, people of color, indigenous people, immigrants, people with accents, people of different religions, and people with disabilities. I think of it this way – everyone has to go to the Department of Motor Vehicles, right? If your staff isn't as diverse as the waiting room of the DMV on a Saturday morning, then you are leaving money on the table in your business.

Let me show you how to go capture it and make the world a better place in the process.

CHAPTER 4

Not a Moment. A Movement

There is a classic dating exercise that I learned from the spiritual teacher, Marianne Williamson way back in my 20s. 'Imagine the person you want to marry. Picture everything. Their clothes, their voice, their job, their values, their job, their education, their body, their laugh. Spare no details. Make the vision as clear as if this person were right in front of you. Then, once you have that image crystal clear in your mind's eye, ask yourself: "Would they date you?"'

The first time I heard this was in a workshop, and the entire room burst out into hysterical laughter at that punch line. Of course they wouldn't! The next part of the workshop was about becoming the person that your ideal mate couldn't resist. In other words, the way to get what you want is to be the person for whom having it is inevitable. Not only true in dating.

Why is it that we expect, or at the very least desire, to be picked out as a diamond in the rough? It's like we want more than we are entitled to, for no good reason. Why would the laws of physics work that way? The truth is, we will be with the partner we are most prepared and aligned to be with. And that, my friends, is true in your business too.

If you want a team of rock stars who are taking total ownership and treating your business like they would treat their own, then you have to be the perfect 10 that your perfect 10 would want to be with.

Alignment Requires Clarity

The traditional millennial approach to work is "I don't care if you pay me a bazillion dollars, I'm not going to lift a finger unless this is a role and a company I am 100% in alignment with." In my opinion this is the cornerstone to having a team that is 100% intrinsically motivated and that works harder and gets better results than any standard operating procedure can generate than any group of primarily boomers or Gen Xers even could. This is because millennials are products of the information age. As a rule, millennials will not be out of alignment for 40+ hours a week is a huge factor that gives me hope in how we, as a planet, will reshape how we think of work postindustrial revolution.

No matter the generation, I don't want anyone on my team who would be willing to be out of alignment in exchange for money. I ask millennials to lead our company because this is so obvious for them, but no matter the age of the person we hire – and we have Gen Y 21-year-olds as well as boomers in their 70s on our team – they must be completely and totally unwilling to compromise their values for a job.

I'm kind of obsessed with this musical called Hamilton by Lin-Manuel Miranda. In the musical, the character of Hamilton says to the character of Aaron Burr, "If you stand for nothing, Burr, what will you fall for?" I need employees who know what they stand for and I need them to be able to tell if we are in alignment with what they stand for or not.

On each page of my website, I have the hashtag #BlackLivesMatter and in our culture guide it says: "Black Lives Matter: I am a social justice activist and while you don't have to be as well, I expect you to respect and demonstrate tolerance for cultural, political, racial, and lifestyle differences in all those you come in contact with. You have a responsibility to understand implicit bias exists and to have some active efforts to acknowledge and address yours."

Most founding CEOs would take the stand that you should leave politics (and religion) out of work. Being professional used to be staying silent on controversy. Millennials have taken that option off the table. If you want a millennial to give 100%, they need to know what they are giving it to. These folx are not dummies, y'all.

Millennials can sniff out integrity from a mile away. If you are saying one thing and doing something else, they casually turn and walk in the other direction.

In order to grow my team, I have had to become much clearer on what our company stands for and who we are, so that candidates who work with us and for us can tell right away, in their gut, if we are energetically aligned or not.

Take religion. We do non-fiction books. Clearly this crosses all faiths and religious beliefs. But my personal beliefs fall into the metaphysical, New Age, woo-woo category. I love crystals and angels and psychics and mediums and all the things that connect us to the great is-that-is. For some people that is just not a fit, doesn't feel good to be around, stifles their creativity, and limits their personal capacity. For those people, The Author Incubator really wouldn't be a good fit.

There was this guy I wanted to bring in to do leadership development and I loved his ideas, but he was super into sports and always used sports metaphors but none of them worked for me because I do not know a thing about sports. And the truth is most of my team doesn't either. So, we didn't hire the guy even though his actual content was great.

There is some other work here that is key which I'm taking for granted you have done. In order to attract great talent, you do need to have a clear mission for your company. You can't expect the employee to figure that out, and not having that foundation will make you unattractive to a prospect.

If you want people to beg to work for you, if you want them to wake up early with a spring in their step and fall asleep thinking about ways to make your dream come true, then you simply owe it to them to know who you are.

We can't expect the sexy someone to come sweep us off our feet if we don't first do the work to be sweep-off-able.

Your Dream Team

In addition to knowing who YOU are, you need to know who your team is. What do they look like? How many people will be on your team in 5 years? What's the age range? Is it a diverse team? Men? Women? Gender non-binary and trans folx? Gay? Straight? Black? White? Brown? Young and malleable? Older and wiser? Combination of the two? I know you THINK you will see what's out there and how it evolves. Let me explain what will happen if you go that way.

You will build a team of people who look like you. Your team will be – about your age, your race, your gender, and your sexual orientation. SURPRISE! This doesn't make you a bad human, but it does make you a reactive one rather than a creative one. If you want a team that doesn't look like you, you have to see that team in advance and you have to create a safe space for those people to see you as their perfect 10.

Let's go back to that dating analogy. Let's say your perfect someone has a super fit athletic body because that's a trait you really enjoy but you are 100 lbs. overweight and totally turned off by going to the gym or for a walk. Well you are going to have a lot of trouble attracting that person with the hot bod into your life. I see this all the time from entrepreneurs. They tell me they want an online business manager to run their business, so they can just tell them what to do and where to show up, but since those entrepreneurs are totally disorganized and don't really demonstrate they value organization, it's hard for a very organized person to thrive in that environment.

When we take this lesson over to differences like race and gender, it's easy to see how our unchecked bias makes someone different than us feel uncomfortable (not safe) on a subconscious level.

When I was growing up, my dad ran a hot rod shop called Total Performance. Hot-rodding, especially in the 80s when I was growing up, was filled with pictures of beautiful cars decorated with naked or almost naked girls. Cars and girls. The industry was almost all men. And when you walked into my dad's shop there were all these hyper-sexualized pictures of cars and girls. If you are a woman coming in for an interview it's going to be hard to feel safe. Of course, women and queer people and people of color have learned how to play it cool and not go screaming out the door when they feel unsafe, but it really does not feel super awesome. If you want to create an amazing team that begs to work for you, it's your responsibility to create a safe place for them. My dad created a safe place for white dudes around his age, and he had a team of those people. If you are happy with having a team like that and it will not negatively affect your revenue goals, go for it. Otherwise, you are going to have to make an effort here.

If you want a diverse client group (and don't forget whites will be in the minority by 2044, according to the Census Bureau) then you have to have a diverse team. And to have a diverse team, you have to create a safe space for diverse employees. You don't create a safe space by being sanitized and generic. You create a safe space by being honest about who you are. If you aren't willing to do the work required to address your unconscious biases, then shout that from the rooftops and plenty of straight white folks will be happy to come running toward another like-minded person. Honestly, I mean this. Imagine if you were a loud and proud white supremacist. How amazing would it feel to have the opportunity to work for an organization that promoted your deepest values? How much harder would you work for that organization than for one that was generic and mealy-mouthed about their values?

I'm obviously not for white supremacy, but, in a weird way, I'd rather see organizations and institutions being honest about who they are and attracting teams that are all-in on their missions. If you are like me and were won over by the arguments of the civil rights movement and if you believe that "all Men are created equal, that they are endowed by their Creator with certain unalienable Rights, that among these are Life, Liberty and the pursuit of Happiness," then I must encourage you to get clear on your commitment to those civil rights. I believe more is required of you than memorizing Martin Luther King, Jr's "I Have a Dream" speech. You must become the person capable of building a company that a diverse group of humans would beg to work for.

What OTHER Problem Does Working for You Solve?

In order to be a company people are begging to work for, working for you has to solve a problem in ADDITION to salary. Salary cannot be the only reason someone works for you, just like hot sex can't be the only reason someone marries you. Maybe it can work for some period of time, but this is not substantial enough to build a relationship. The job has to also be doing something else.

Think about the problem working for one of the top white-shoe law firms solves for a law school grad. Yes, it pays the bills. Yes, the student loans will get paid off. But the bigger problem working for White & Case or Sullivan & Cromwell solves is one of moral pride. It answers the question "Was it worth it to spend all that time and money on law school?" with a resounding external "Yes!" Humans worry "Did I just waste 3 years and $200K on law school?" That's normal and natural. A job someone begs for is a job that solves more than money.

Part of your mission before you start the hiring process is to identify which problems you can solve for people. Here are a few examples of problems we solve for our employees (other than giving them a paycheck, which they could get anywhere). These are quite possibly not the problems working for your business would solve, and that's okay. The point is, you need to know what problems working for you does solve.

1. Ability to work from home so that I can balance school drop-offs, pick-ups, holidays, and sick days with my work
2. Ability to set my own work schedule so I can help my aging and ill parent
3. Ability to own my training and experience as a healer without being embarrassed about my lack of desire to do all the entrepreneurial stuff needed to build a business
4. Ability to read and work on books on topics I am most interested in
5. Ability to get frequent paid trips to Washington, DC, where I have lots of friends
6. Ability to fund my artistic endeavors in a way that feels aligned to my greater purpose

What is the dream that working for your company can help someone achieve? You can't know that if you don't have a very clear vision and identity for who your company is and what types of people you want to call into it.

Step 1 Conclusion: Cultivate Controversy

In this chapter we learned how you have to first be the company that your ideal employees would want to work for. Take stock of how you are doing that today.

1. Do you have a mission, vision, and values that a REASONABLE person could totally DISagree with? (If not, write one!)
2. Have you created a safe space for people who look like the clients or customers you want to work? (If not, get on it!)
3. Finally, do you know what problem working for your company will solve for your dream employees. (If not, dream employees will be working somewhere else. Do it!)

CHAPTER 5

There Is No Bus (#sorrynotsorry)

What's that business book everyone recommends? Good to Great? Do you know it? The author, Jim Collins, has this thing about getting the right people on the bus, the wrong people off the bus, and the right people in the right seats. It's an awesome visual, but it's fucking dumb. You know why? There is no bus!

My business changes so fast the idea of getting the right people in the right seats is just silliness. People change and the business changes. Are there wrong people who need to be quickly shown the door? Yup, for sure, but the idea there are right people and right seats is so much tidier than I have found real life to be.

The best you can do is capture your org chart at a point in time. You job isn't to figure out what the bus is, who the right people are, or what their seats are. Your job is to figure out what is the most urgent problem in your business today that hiring someone can solve.

As an author coach, I advise solopreneurs and micro-business owners who don't have enough time to get everything done. Essentially, they feel like they need to duplicate themselves because there isn't enough to go around. When they hire, they (often subconsciously) try to find people just like themselves to take on the things they are supposed to be getting done, but it never quite works out. This is because most entrepreneurs are thinking about "help" too broadly. You can't "replace yourself" or "clone yourself" – that's not a thing. Instead, you need to break up all the things you do and hire multiple people to each do part of what you as the founder were capable of.

You Can't Clone Yourself. That's Not a Thing.

Let me save you some effort, the cloning yourself plan will not work. No one, is ever going to come close to doing this job as well as you, or even adequately. The best you can hope for is to find people who will do discrete parts of your job BETTER than you and for that to happen – the organization itself needs to keep continually evolving into something totally new.

When Rae Guyn joined our team, I needed more time. I needed to start getting myself out of administrative tasks like uploading recordings to the cloud, or collecting client questions, or printing handouts for events. I needed an assistant. Rae proved herself more than adequate at assisting but I noticed something within a few months. Rae made me feel safe. And when I felt safe, I noticed, I was so much better at the things clients really paid for. Clients were most definitely not willing to pay for someone to upload a video or make a photocopy, but for me to be in my zone of genius downloading messages from the universe to whisper (or scream) directly into client's ears? That could get a lined queued up around the block.

Rae's zone of genius is bringing order to chaos, calm to the storm, love to the fight. Rae creates a sense of trust among anyone in the room with her in a way I never will, even if I spent hours each week trying to improve this task.

As the owner of the business I had given myself so many jobs, I couldn't possibly be good at them. Coaching? Writing? Strategizing? Check. Check. Check. Administrative logistics? Creating Safe Spaces? Brining Calm to the Chaos? Yeah... not so much.

So why would I want a CLONE when I had RAE?!?!?

What I needed was more time doing what I was good at, and Rae spending more time doing what she was good at. A team of clones would lead to defeat. It would be a room full of disorganized smart people. That and $5 will get you a Latte!

Tedious, But Powerful Task List

The way I recommend growing your team is tedious, but incredibly powerful and it's the same for solopreneurs and small companies. Have everyone in the company (just you if that's all there is) make a ridiculously exhausting list of everything they do. This will 100% seem impossible if you are doing it right. My favorite technique is going through sent email and calendar appointments to remind myself of what I've completed.

One of my team members did this assignment over a week writing down and categorizing everything she did and eventually lumping some of them together into the same activity. I do want to show you her list but it's 187 tasks long! So, it will not read well. But I'll share a few of the items from the list:

1. Systemizing the packets for editor friendliness
2. Monitor, update, and improve packets

3. Assign editors to authors
4. Determine the talking points for the trimester 2 intro call
5. Spot check trimester 2 intro calls and update talking points if needed
6. Create course correction dos and don'ts checklist
7. Monitor managing editor course correction
8. Have weekly calls with managing editor to review each author
9. Have team report emergencies to head of customer experience
10. Revise RCR welcome message
11. Create quality score for TAW manuscripts and RCR books
12. Hire proofreaders
13. Review and improve proofreaders

The next step is to give yourself a ranking on each of these tasks. Basically, you are going to give yourself an A, B, or C. A grade of a C means you can do it but you are barely competent, you kind of suck – it gets done, but it's not amazing and drains you of your life force. A grade of a B means you are pretty good at it and you don't mind doing it at all. You might not be the best in the world at it, but it's pretty satisfying, and while there are better people in the world at it, you're not so bad at it, especially since the process of finding someone better at it seems long and hard. A grade of an A means it's 100% what you were put on this earth to do. This is your sweet spot and finding someone to do this task better than you will be a needle in the haystack search because you are one of the best in the world.

For now, you are required to do all the jobs – whether you rate yourself an A, B, or C. These are all passing grades. We do want to make sure any tasks you or someone on your team is out right failing gets taken away from them. Usually this is easy because we don't like to keep tasks we totally fail at. For instance, I'm terrible at graphic design so even though I did almost every job in my company, I've always outsourced cover design, even when I couldn't afford to, because I am 100% incompetent at book cover design. I get an F. Hiring people for things you are completely miserable at (even if you don't have the money to hire someone) is remarkably easy. The problem is hiring someone for the tasks you are good at, but not the best at (the Bs).

Find the Gaps

Once you have completed lists for everyone in your company you will see a massive list of tasks. Sort them by grade. First priority, without delay, is to hire staff or vendors for any tasks anyone on your team is totally failing at, or to give those tasks to current staff who are better at them. There should be relatively few of these.

Now look at the remaining bullet points. Great news! All that work was worth the effort. These are the basis for all your future job descriptions! We will cover how to write job descriptions in the next chapter, but having these bullet-pointed tasks is essential to that process.

Sort all the bullet points rated B and C into a single document and begin to see how many jobs those tasks can be broken into at the MAXIMUM. You won't go from no employees doing the job to the maximum. It will be a slow and steady progression. As you do this task, don't worry about salaries or where the money will come from, just sort the roles and the tasks that job is responsible for.

Our goal here is to start seeing the future and which are the tasks that are most critical that we are lacking excellence in. This is going to show you where you need to hire. Sometimes if you are feeling blocked here it can help to start by making a list of what you do and putting a star by the tasks you love most and are absolutely required for and wouldn't want to give up. Ultimately, we want 80% of your time and all of your team's time spent on things they would get an A on.

Focus Everyone on Their Strengths

I first learned this concept from a book called StrengthsFinder. The idea was that most of us identify our weaknesses in school and through our work evaluations and feedback from managers and we work on improving our weaknesses, but what if, instead, we focused on improving our STRENGTHS. It's counterintuitive, but you can QUICKLY get much better at your strengths whereas it's really hard and slow to get even a little better at your weaknesses. Focusing on your strengths has a lot more upside and a lot less downside.

By knowing your zone of genius – the things you get an A on – you have a huge upper hand as you decide what roles to hire for first. Start by hiring in your zone of competence, your Cs. Those will be easy to give up and almost anyone who wants those tasks can do better than you do with them so you will be easily pleased. See if you can group all your Cs into a single job or maybe 2 or 3 depending on how many there are or how many B tasks are tangentially related.

The most common first jobs I see hired out are domestic tasks like cooking and cleaning, and administrative work like post office runs and bill paying. The next level is usually technical tasks like web coding or design. And then advertising, marketing, and sales. Usually the last tasks to be given away are either service delivery or product creation related.

Your first task to having a team that is thrilled, delighted, aligned, and on fire to help you build your dream is to create the organization chart of your future. Decide everyone you are going to hire in 3 years (it will be all wrong, by the way) and then put dates next to each hire. For each hire you need about $200,000 to $300,000 in revenue, so if your revenue is growing by $500K a year, then you are probably looking at 2 new hires a year. The org chart is not a bus. It will continue to mold and shape and grow, but it's so helpful to see where you are going because as you hire, having that vision for what growth can look like for your new employee is essential. You want to be able to pull out the org chart in your interview and point to where they are starting and what position they could be in in 3 years. When you have your 3-year org chart it gives your candidates confidence that you are going to be around, that there is a plan, and, most importantly, that this isn't just a business transaction but the beginning of a relationship.

Step 2 Conclusion: Operate into the Future
Once you have done the tedious and time-consuming work in this chapter, you will have a 3-year hiring plan that will morph and grow and change as your needs and your network do.

1. Are you willing to commit a week of focus to identifying all the tasks in your business? (If so, which week? Pick it now.)
2. When you identify tasks that are a B or a C for you or a team member, are you willing create a position for those tasks for the future even if you can't see how you can pay for it now? (When you do this, you will change the energy you or the team member has around doing this task since it's now only temporary!)
3. Finally, based on your list of jobs and tasks for each job, are you willing to create an organizational chart for the future to

build toward? (Remember your goal is to be someone's dream come true. For you to create a dream come true job you need to have a clear vision of where you are going and who you want to take on the journey.)

CHAPTER 6

If You Only Read One Chapter, Make It This One

"I want to do something crazy with our job description for this role.... I know you are going to yell at me, but have a read. I think it will weed out candidates I don't want to work with anyway."

Those were the words I shared with my friend and super-recruiter Daphne Boyd when I got the idea that the standard job description needed to go the way of the dodo bird. Daphne did not agree.

She replied:

"I've heard you say weed out a few times and I'm on alert because the goal here should be to attract the right person to your company. I think the approach should be deliver your messaging with balance. Too much wow factor can turn away solid suitors. The Job Description is there to convey your company's required skills sought. Its only job is to define the expectation required for the position. Some traditions may be boring but a necessary evil. We will ultimately handle this the way you'd like but I'd like you to remember that we can get that creative, innovative culture conveyed without scaring them away first."

I knew what she meant. Daphne has always been the good girl in our friendship. Don't get me wrong, she gets her way, but she does it by mostly playing by the rules. I knew she would hate the job description I put together. It had swears, bad grammar, strange punctuation, and a funny bit in the middle about numerology. It was bad enough I was running an unknown startup. The crazy-ass job description was not going to make finding the right candidate any easier.

And, who knows, maybe Daphne's approach is the right one for your organization and you should stick with the traditional job post. If that is the case, there are plenty of books and reference tools out there for you and this chapter will be of no use to you. But if you have been less than thrilled with the quality of candidates that show up for jobs you post, you might want to try a different approach.

This is a whole new way to find the perfect person to fill the role you have open but it's based on the tried and true art of direct response marketing. Since defying my friend and posting that first description, we've gotten tons more applications for each position, we only have to read a few, we interview 1 or maybe 2 people, and we always quickly hire a perfect match.

In this chapter I'm going to teach you my process for writing a job description that calls in the most amazing prospective employees. In the previous chapter you should have pinpointed which job you are going to fill first. Now, let's take your vision for the company and merge it with that job description to create a powerful magnet for your perfect person to find you. I am going to warn you again this is total ninja shit, so if you take one punch or kick out of the system and try to apply it inside the traditional approach it will likely backfire on you. Use this system with extreme caution.

The Philosophy Behind the Approach

Most job ads, including the ones Daphne wanted to write, are designed to "convey your company's required skills sought," or at least that has been the way it's worked until now. The person with the power in the relation is me, the job description writer. I'm the one with the money, so I'm the one who is going to get what I want. I have the problem and you – person I pay – is going to solve my problem in exchange for cold, hard cash. Yeah. Nope. Not how it works with millennials.

Hegel wrote about the master/slave dialectic. What Hegel was saying was inside of each of us we are both the master and the slave, depending on the circumstance and the view of the other person we're relating to. Understanding of who we are is always viewed through the mirror of who is asking. Is the employer the master or the slave?

Hegel has a twist (one which Karl Marx was a huge fan of). He said (and I'm seriously over-simplifying here) the real power the employer has is that the employee is willing to agree the worker is the slave. But the truth is the employer is dependent on the labor of the employee. Neither can be considered entirely a slave or a master. As the employer, I can be viewed as the master, but in many ways I am also the slave to that employee's willingness to be employed. (Queer folx like me sometimes call this topping from the bottom.) Evolution requires me to see the master/slave dialectic between an employee and employer is a false distinction, or at least a social construct that isn't very helpful.

In fact, Hegel proves over and over that these power dynamics (asymmetric recognitive relations, as he calls them) are metaphysically defective or, as I like to call it – fucked up. It gives all the power to the employer and then the employer is in this prison of their own making while the same is true for the employee, who takes on the role of slave. Hegel's argument is that unless authority and responsibility are equal, shit is going to keep being fucked up (he doesn't use those exact words).

The philosophy behind the "make 'em beg" technique is to disrupt the master/slave dialectic, turning the tables so that the master is the prospective employee, and then turning them back again to even the playing field. By acknowledging this is a fair, equal, and symbiotic relationship (aka, we need each other equally) it completely changes the energy moving from the job description to the application stage.

Watch carefully as we go from master to slave in the job description process. This is part of why you can't just take one piece of the five steps and put it into your job description and make it work. When we get to Part 3, you will see what I mean – there is a clever idea you will want to adopt but it won't really be effective on its own in your more standard job description.

What Is Your Ideal Candidate's Problem and Dream Come True?

There are 5 parts to the job description itself and I will explain each part of the process below, but before you get to those 5 parts, we need to know who your ideal candidate is so we can write the job description like a love letter straight to their heart. It's probably helpful to understand the origins of this approach are based in the direct response marketing sales letter technique. Direct response marketing was started in the 1960s and is often associated with Ron Popeil and the Ginsu knife, but the approach I take in my job descriptions is much softer. The thing it has in common is that I am very clear about what problem my job solves for the reader of the ad who is looking for work, and what dream come true they will have if they choose to solve their problem by applying for and getting this job.

Before you start writing the actual job description, you will want to reflect back on that vision you had for your whole team 3 years from now. Picture an actual person very vividly. In fact, I recommend finding a picture of a person who looks like the person who is going to fill the role. Do they use a wheel chair? Is their hair blonde? Do they have a funky fashion sense? I know it seems weird, but I want you to see an actual person with an actual name, age, address – all the actual demographics any single actual human has. When I set out to fill any role, I picture an Ideal Candidate for the person I want to come find me to fill the role. It's just a journal entry with almost a character sketch of who this person is.

I can see the whole person in my mind's eye. Where they went to school. Their favorite vacation spot. Their living situation. Their current job. All of it.

Now, please know I'm not RIGHT about any of it – it's all made up in my mind's eye, but I make it very, very, very specific, so it's like this is an actual person. When I do this, the person naturally has some problems. The problems come out in the journal entry and become the basis for my job description. (Note that skipping this step will make all the other steps totally ineffective.)

In this step my main goal is to identify the problem and dream come true this job is going to solve for the Ideal Candidate. It doesn't mean I have the problem and dream come true correct for the actual person I'm going to hire, but it means when I go to write the job description I will be able to be very specific, which is one of the keys to making direct response marketing work.

Consider Ron Popeil's pitch for the Chop-O-Matic hand food processor. He said, "Ladies and gentlemen, I'm going to show you the greatest kitchen appliance ever made…. All your onions chopped to perfection without shedding a single tear." He didn't say, "It's going to chop anything that needs chopping real good." He was specific about the PROBLEM of crying when you cut onions. Now, even if you are allergic to onions and never slice them, you get the idea – anything can be chopped, but this pitch is so much better because it's more specific.

Also, while we are at it, when it comes to chopping vegetables, what's my dream come true? That they will chop themselves, of course! That's why the name Chop-O-Matic is so brilliant. The name itself IS the dream come true. That is why the job title is so important.

Part 1: The Title Is Not the Title

This might seem counter-intuitive, but instead of making the title for the job that is featured in the ad, the actual title, make it the title your dream candidate is most likely to search on the job board. The purpose of the Job Ad Title is to get your ideal reader's attention. If the title is cutesy or clever or just company-specific, it can't be the Job Ad Title for a "make 'em beg" ad. You need to picture your ideal candidate searching on the job board – what job title would they search for – and then picture them telling their mom or their spouse or their best friend that they are so excited about applying for this job, and they have to be able to say the title and immediately get the approval of their loved one.

If your ideal candidate graduated from law school, is taking the Bar Exam, and wants a first-year associate job, calling your position Legal Happiness Guru is not going to fly. You are going to want to go with Associate Attorney. Yes, even if you are disrupting the legal industry. You just can't introduce that level of confusion to the Job Ad Title.

I have a position called Developmental Editor, but the way we do the job, it's very much a marketing strategy role, so I've advertised the job as a Marketing Director and Marketing Strategist, and even as Creative Director, because the dream come true for my Ideal Candidate before she finds out about me is one of those jobs. That's how her alerts and auto email notifications are set up and that's what she is searching for on Indeed and LinkedIn. They are definitely not searching for Developmental Editor. I know this because when I posted the ad with that title I got literary fiction candidates who didn't groove to my marketing jive at all.

Your job title reflects the title your ideal candidate is SEARCHING for on the job sites. You can explain in the interview stage if that's not the job title you are offering.

Write the title for the first position you are going to fill.

Part 2: Problem and Dream Come True

Since most job descriptions are written from the perspective of the employer as master and the problem the master has, this gets the entire relationship off to the wrong start. Employers need employees just as much as employees need employers. We are both masters and both slaves. In order to make it clear you understand this, you want to start your job description from the perspective of the reader. Don't worry – we will get to your problems later. For now, what is the problem your ideal candidate has? As you read the opening paragraphs for 3 of our job descriptions, see if you can picture in your mind's eye the ideal candidate I was writing it to.

Here's the Title (part 1) and the Problem and Dream Come True (Part 2) of one of the positions we hire for regularly:

Managing Editor

GET PAID TO READ NON-FICTION BOOKS! (Really!)

If that sounds like a "too good to be true" dream job for you, keep reading.

Most editors only get paid to read half the time. They spend most of the time managing clients, trying to find clients, dealing with unhappy clients, invoicing clients, and a ton of other administrivia that would drive anyone to reconsider their career choice if their real passion was reading books.

You probably started editing because you enjoyed helping people turn their ideas into impactful words – but how much time do you spend doing that? And when you DO get to do that, do you find your feedback isn't always met with appreciation?

Most editors say that all too often their clients question their expertise and pile on irrational request after irrational request, all while treating them like they are barely human. Of course as the editor, you have to sit there and take it because "the customer is always right."

What if you didn't have these problems? What if you could get paid to read? What if every single client was grateful for your advice, had perfect boundaries with you, respected your time and talent, and never tried to barter or bargain

Do you see how this would be the problem and dream come true of the ideal candidate for managing editor at The Author Incubator?

Here are the Titles and Problem/Dream Come True statements for a few other roles at our company.

Junior Editor/Editorial Intern

Every good editor had to get their start somewhere, right? Someone gave them a break or at least a chance to get their hands on manuscripts and show what they could do to improve it. We want to give that chance to our next entry level employee in our growing and dynamic editorial team.

IT Specialist

At this point, you would think the technically gifted would get more respect in society considering how much we all rely on our phones, computers, and online systems these days; but, alas, the nerdy computer-geek stereotype persists. Maybe you fit the part and own your place behind a hand-assembled Windows OS PC, or maybe you are a little different – the chocolate of your skin or the curve of your waist betraying the typical mold.

While you are happy to hide behind the glow of high-frequency electromagnetic waves, you are also ready to be seen and recognized for the full and complete human you are. Yes, naturally gifted with technology, but so much more than a computer geek.

The Author Incubator is waiting for you to come shine in your own quirky way over here as our IT Specialist.

Write 1 to 3 paragraphs describing your ideal candidate's problem and dream come true.

Part 3: Responsibilities with a Twist

The actual job description part is where you list the duties from the previous chapter's list of tasks. These are the bullet-pointed list of your B- and C-grade tasks that you know you need to stop doing. We are hiring to get these tasks off your plate. These bullet points can be very matter of fact.

Here are ours for a job on our finance team:

Preferred Requirements

- Knowledge of and interest in personal development and the experts industry
- Comfortable talking on the phone with clients and team members several hours a day
- An accounting degree is preferred but not a must, along with experience in accounts payable and reconciliation
- Knowledge of basic bookkeeping and QuickBooks
- Min. 2 - 4 years bookkeeping experience
- Pride in accuracy and fastidious attention to detail
- Upbeat, organized self-starter able to work in a dynamic environment with limited oversight
- Excellent written and verbal communication skills
- Ability to meet deadlines and promptly respond to requests

- Favorably represent the company to customers

And here they are for a web designer job:

We are looking for someone to:

- Design high-converting, aesthetically beautiful designs that comply with brand standards and guidelines
- Develop graphics for multiple channels, including social media, email, web, and print
- Create new web pages and update website(s) in WordPress
- Continually optimize all our web offers' performance and assist in evolving our website strategy
- Manage and maintain digital asset library using shared services like Box and Basecamp.
- Create compelling PowerPoint presentations that communicate mood, emphasis, insight, viewpoint, and similar visual impressions, to convey ideas and information clearly

The tricky part here is not the responsibilities themselves – the lists above are both different in style, but will service the job post fine. There is only one more thing you need to add to make this a "make 'em beg" ad, and that is a secret code.

You will insert into the middle of the list of bullet points a secret code. Here's how I do mine, and I put it RIGHT in the middle of all the bullets; that way I know they read the description.

- Random bullet point inserted to see if you are paying attention. Put the secret code number 47 in your application email subject line, k? Thx.

The secret code alone won't really work if you don't follow this whole process, but it's incredibly powerful in limiting the number of bad applications you need to sort through, for sure.

Grab your bullet points from the exercise in the last chapter and turn them into job-ad-friendly bullet points with a random secret code bullet point right in the middle before you go on to the next section.

Part 4: Process to Apply

The magic of the "make 'em beg" approach is really here in Part 4. Here is where we switch back into the alpha role and tell the prospect what to do and how to do it. In this section of the job ad I give them 3 to 4 very specific steps. I make it clear that I am, in fact, the prize in this scenario, and that the prize never chases. If the prospect would like the prize, they are going to have to do some things my way. Of course the PRIZE itself is an egalitarian work place that makes a huge difference for its clients, is in alignment and integrity, has a clear and outspoken set of values, and sees you as an equal in the master/slave dialect. So it's an ironic prize because as soon as you claim it you become a part of the prize. Still, it's very clear you as the prospect are going to chase us and not the other way around, which is extremely important. Our entire philosophy with clients and employees is that the prize never chases, and if something isn't a fit there is never drama, just a simple recognition that it is not working and we are adults and should move on.

What I'm communicating on a subconscious level here is "Hey, listen, this is your life, which you are the master of, but it's also my business, which I am the master of. Sometimes this will be about my needs and sometimes it will be about yours. What do you think?"

Now, of course, except for the philosophy students in the room, no one really gets what's happening, but for many people they aren't comfortable with the grey area that doesn't play by traditional, old school, hard-and-fast, patriarchy-inspired rules about who is the master and who is the slave. For those folks, these instructions will seem overwhelming, or boring, or confusing. And that is precisely what we want to happen. Those are the droids, not who you are looking for.

Here's how this part of the job description reads:

We will likely get 200+ resumes for this role and we just don't have time to interview many candidates, so make this stand out if you want a job that will change the entire trajectory of your life.

Instructions:

(1) Email us a resume at Work@TheAuthorIncubator.com along with a cover letter or video (video is strongly preferred).

(2) In your cover letter or video include your compensation requirements. (Note, be strategic here. If you pick a number in the range we have in mind, and everything else in your application looks good, we will interview you. If you shoot too high and pick a number outside of our range and you would have been happy with a lower number, we won't get the chance to talk, even if the rest of your appli-

cation is perfect. And if you don't provide a number at all, we will completely dismiss your application. We do not provide the range in advance. We want to hear what the lowest number is that would make the job a hell yes for you if all the other conditions were met.)

(3) Tell us how you will fit in THIS job specifically. We know what's a fit for us and we want to know if this is a fit for YOU. We will NOT be calling you to clarify whether or not you're a fit. SELL US on why we would be lucky to have you on the team.

(4) Make sure your email subject line has the secret code in it. If you don't have the secret code, please do not apply.

Your turn! Write your instructions for applicants. Make sure you require the secret code in the subject line and make it clear you are the prize.

Part 5: Who We Are / Our Values

After we give the instructions I always say a little more about who we are and our values. You don't have to do this part, especially if diversity isn't a core value for you, but it's something that helps us signal to our candidates we are doing our best to create a safe space for all sorts of candidates. I will tell you that I personally believe the very best candidates are often the ones who don't feel safe applying, and standard, government, or lawyer-approved diversity statements will not make them feel any safer.

We had this candidate the other day who blew me away. He was clearly extremely gifted and was managing MS as a stay-at-home dad. He made a great video from his chair, with some speech challenges, and I thought to myself, "Holy shit. How brave do you have to be to make a video when sending a letter would allow you to hide?" It made me proud of myself for creating a safe space and, like, 10 times more interested in him as a candidate because of how much grit he had and how much personal work was behind the clarity and confidence in that video. But those videos don't come unless you do the work first.

Diversity isn't about how you interview or about salary distribution – it starts with examining the bias around pronouns, gender, sexual orientation, and skin color in your job descriptions. And it continues to the thought and care and heart in your diversity statement.

Here's our diversity statement. I wrote it after the 2018 mid-term elections.

One thing you should know about us. Our organization believes in diversity and equity. You know those 112 women and 117 People of Color in Congress now? Yup, still not nearly enough for us. We put muscle behind our values when it comes to building an inclusive community for staff and clients. We believe EQUITY (not just inclusion) is what really is required to dismantle racism and patriarchy. We are an LGBTQIA-affirming, interfaith-oriented organization that is committed to social justice – including women's rights, civil rights, disability rights, immigrant rights, and environmental justice. We believe Black Lives Matter. We encourage candidates to apply who share these commitments and who have a demonstrated capacity for creating inclusive organizations and working effectively across differences to support the success of an increasingly diverse clientele. (In other words, we don't work with racist, homophobic, transphobic, misogynistic jerks.)

Here's a less elaborate diversity statement I used before that election.

Please note: We are an LGBTQIA-affirming, interfaith-oriented organization. We are committed to social justice, including women's rights, civil rights, disability rights, immigrant rights, and environmental justice. We believe Black Lives Matter. We encourage candidates to apply who share these commitments and who have a demonstrated capacity for creating inclusive organizations and working effectively across differences to support the success of an increasingly diverse clientele.

Are you going to add a diversity statement? If so, write yours now. Make sure it's true and honest for you.

Step 3 Conclusion: Market to Your Prospective Workers

I think the most important thing for you to know about job descriptions is that it's not about solving your problem in filling the role, it's about the ideal candidate solving theirs. If you can be a giver in this part of the process the quality of your candidates will go through the roof.

1. Did you follow the steps in the 5 parts above and write your first job description the make 'em beg way? (If not, do it now!)
2. Read back through your job description and as you read it can you imagine your ideal candidate being pulled toward you almost magnetically? (If so, that's the power of direct response marketing

3. Finally, I know there is a lot here in this chapter and I want to make it easy for you so I'm putting all my job descriptions into a single document that you can download totally free at www.TheAuthorIncubator.com/JDs.

CHAPTER 7

You Had Me at Hello

The purpose of the Job Posting, which you should post on any job-posting websites that strike your fancy, is to get you extremely high-quality candidates who are excited to show you why they should be allowed into your club. The purpose of this chapter is to help you navigate from a few great candidates to a filled role. Most organizations focus on the interview, but the interview is actually everything that happens after you find an interesting candidate until the minute they sign on the dotted line.

If the secret code is not in the subject line of the emails you receive from a prospective employee, do yourself a favor and hit delete without opening. Accepting a candidate who doesn't follow instructions during the application process will only lead to heartache later. The interview starts right there. If the candidate isn't willing to follow your lead on that one, you can't be surprised when they don't follow as the asks get more complex. An employee is not likely to be MORE compliant than a candidate.

For those applications that have the secret code, make sure all aspects of the instructions have been addressed. One of the main components here is the salary request. We'll talk about salary in a future chapter, but for now know that it's essential your candidate shares their salary requirement in the reply and that the requirement is in the range (or below the range) you have available. The problem with negotiating a different salary is you now know how much they really want to make and if it's less than you are offering you know they will be looking for other opportunities.

The Screening Begins

Only send candidates on to the next round that have the secret code and a salary that works. If they've got both of those things and there are no other red flags in their application, the next step is a quick phone screening. It's important you do not schedule this. Instead just text first and say something like, "Hey, this is Angela from The Author Incubator. I'm looking at your application for editor and have a couple questions. Can I give you a quick call?"

Most people will get confused here and focus on the questions (and sure, there are questions you will ask) but the main point of this part of the interview is to see if the candidate will drop everything to talk with you. It won't determine if they get the job, but it's worth noting how hungry they are for the position. Remember, the prize never chases.

The stated purpose of the phone screening is to assign a written project. Again, don't get confused by what the written project is, or even how well the candidate performs the task. What we want to measure is WHO this person is and HOW they will behave.

I have a PhD in the social sciences and one of the things I studied is the use of pornography in the diffusion of innovations. Pornography is a tricky topic to do qualitative research around because just about everybody is going to lie about it. But it's not just pornography people lie about, it's pretty much everything. When you ask a candidate "how will you handle this situation" in an interview setting they are going to answer what they think you want to hear. It will be a version of the truth but not the whole truth.

Instead, put them in a situation and see what they do. You are observing them in their natural environment. This IS the interview. When you get on the phone with them you are testing the real answer to the question, "how big of a priority is this job to you" or "if there is something important at work that happens when you have another conflict, how will you handle it." When you give the written project, you are testing the real answer to the question "do you like to take you time with a project and mull it over, or do it quickly?" and "do you like to ask a lot of questions before you do a project or just dive in?"

Different roles require different skills and approaches, but when you ASK for self-reported data, that data will always be skewed. When you observe the facts, you can get a much more realistic picture of what it will be like to work with this person.

The interview itself is the LEAST important part of the hiring process from candidate to employee. Before that even happens though you want to confirm what you believe from the application. Check to make sure you are agreed on the working location, the salary, and just the general vibe. Here we are looking for any other red flags that make the interviewer uncomfortable. It can be hard to discern a weird personality from nerves, but that's part of what you need to be assessing.

The basic structure of the phone screen goes like this

1. Text to see if they are free but also to test their level of excitement and interest with the job
2. Jump on a call quickly, unscheduled on the pretense of confirming the basic data in the application, but really listen for red flags or signs this is a soulmate. Here is where you key into your intuition
3. If the candidate seems like a potential fit, assign a project in small part to see the quality or substance of their work but in larger measure to see the STYLE of their work

The Written Project

At the end of the phone screening, if the hiring manager wants to move the candidate further into the process they will give them an assignment. The assignment should be created to test for the candidate's ability to do the job but secretly there is another agenda. My life coach trainer, Martha Beck, said, "The way we do anything is the way we do everything." I have found this to be totally true. While you do want to make sure candidates pass the basic content of the assignment, the real purpose is to watch the "how" of it all. Hiring managers should pay attention to how the candidate acts during the entire process – not just the assignment content but how they execute the assignment, how fast they get the assignment back, how excited they are, how many questions they ask, etc. If they give excuses or are late, that is a sign they are not a fit. If they ask questions in a way that annoys you now, it's not going to get any better later.

You want to create an assignment that should reasonably take 2 to 4 hours to complete. The maximum time you want to give for this assignment is 72 hours. If they can't find 2 to 4 hours in the next 72 hours, they don't really want the job. That's basically the equivalent of cancelling a dinner or having a doctor's appointment. If that deadline isn't met, the candidate should be abandoned. No extensions, no excuses. Remember, it's not really about the assignment; it's about the "how," so it doesn't make sense to give an extension or accept an excuse, because that's the very thing we are testing – do they ask for extensions or give excuses?

The basic structure of the written test goes like this:

1. Verbally communicate the test over the phone. It doesn't matter what it is but it's easiest if it's an assignment the person in this role will do regularly. For our book cover designers, they designer a book cover, for our editors, they edit a chapter, for our IT folks, they create a migration plan. Tell them on the phone what they will do and that the due date will be no more than 72 hours from when you are talking. Get a verbal commitment they are in.

2. Send a write up of the assignment with any supporting materials as well as the due date for the assignment and get a written confirmation. (Don't say this but

the hope is usually that the assignment will be submitted sooner than the due date.)
3. Observe everything about how the assignment is handled. Are questions asked? Should they have been? Does the assignment come in early? Late? Does the candidate make excuses? This is pretty shocking but we see about 50% of candidates ghost right at this point- which tells us what they would be like as a colleague. Yes, sure, look at the assignment. The quality doesn't NOT matter, but as long as the quality is coachable, it's the least important part

The Interview

If the candidate passes the assignment portion of the process, the next step is to schedule an interview. This should happen ideally within 24 hours of receiving the assignment. The interview should happen with the hiring manager and any other decision-makers/informers. The interview is the time to ask the candidate, "What are you looking for in a job?"

An ideal candidate is one who can articulate an answer to questions about how this job will facilitate their personal goals. Look for the win-win beyond salary. I have seen how people are being trained to do job interviews now and it's not really what I'm personally looking for. I do sometimes go through their resume quickly just to break the ice, but mostly I'm trying to get them to be an actual human with me and not a performative being. I ask them to tell me about their favorite person on the planet, what makes them smile, what pisses them off. Again, I'm just trying to see the real person that way.

During the interview the hiring manager should confirm the start date and salary expectations. If the candidate is not a fit, then end the interview or tell them they aren't a fit. It's always best to do this live, but you can send an email if needed.

The purpose of the interview is to understand how – beyond a paycheck – this job will serve the candidate. If the employer is the slave and not the master after all, what will we have to do to keep our master happy?

The basic structure of the interview goes like this:

1. Have a face-to-face in person or over video meeting where you get the candidate to specifically answer what they are looking for in a job and how this job fits that role.
2. Ask the candidate what they learned from the interview process that made them question if this was the right company or the right role.
3. Finally ask the candidate to explain, beyond money, how this job helps them reach their most significant personal goal that they can identify. (This goal should be something like having a baby, falling in love, writing a novel, buying a dream house or moving to Croatia. We are looking for built in/integrated/integral "work-life" balance. Since work is a part of your life, we want to make

sure work is supporting your whole life not just the mental stimulation or the financial necessity parts. I want to know the candidate as a whole person.)

Closing the Deal & Salary Negotiation

If the candidate is a fit, then let them know: "This feels like a fit to me. Based on what we discussed, is there anything that gives you reason for concern? Are there any questions I can answer?" If you are making the offer alone you can present the offer letter right then. If not, let them know you need to review with your team, but everything looks good and you will reach out as soon as possible to schedule a meeting with some others, as needed.

This is the point where you will want to review the salary. Pull out their offer letter and agree to give them exactly what they asked for. Then agree that if after 90 days the employee is fully ramped up and contributing to the team that you will give them a raise. We actually do a 5-10% raise there and that's what I recommend to you if you have a Rockstar. Going out to recruit a new candidate for that role will cost at least that much. A recruiter would cost twice that much. So if you have a winner, let them know it with a raise at 3 months and tell them when you make the offer that's what will happen.

Run through all the other benefits at this point if there are any. When you present the offer letter it's really important the offer is fully explained in context of the candidate's personal dream come true. It's not about the job or the salary; it's about getting their other personal victory (their golden why) through this job. This is a sales pitch. They are buying into your dream with their time and life force. The salary offsets that but don't be confused – the person making the big investment is the employee not the employer. After going through the terms of the agreement the key question to ask is, "Is there any reason in your mind right now that might make this a no for you?" If there is, you want that out on the table so you can address it while you are together.

The candidate should have no longer than 24 hours to respond to the offer. If they are saying they need time to give notice and it's a Friday – I still wouldn't extend that. If they aren't busting out of their skin with excitement to sign the contract it is honestly probably not a good fit. No one should want more than 24 hours to sign. Think of it this way, if Beyoncé asked them to work for her, how long would they need to decide?

The total target timing from application received to hiring is one week. The number 1 goal is to move fast. The best candidates will want to get the deal done and get to work.

If the candidate leaves the interview unsure or gets confused in the hours that follow, trust the universe that this is a sign this is not your person and let them go with love. I always say to candidates at this point it should feel like you are getting offered a job with Beyoncé. If you need more time to think about it, it probably means it isn't really a fit.

The basic structure of making an offer goes like this:

1. Ask if there are any reasons if the salary matches what they said they wanted that knowing what they know now they would not accept the offer. Do not make an offer until or unless you get a yes on this question.
2. Once you get a yes, offer the exact salary they asked for with a planned raise at the 90-day mark if certain goals are met. Share any other benefits at this time as well.
3. Only give a maximum of 24 hours to decide if it's a yes or a no. Do not negotiate any terms except something like start date by a day or two at this point. If they don't feel like they won the lottery to work for you, this is not your person! Move on!

Step 4 Conclusion: Pick the winners

We need all the hiring heavy lifting to happen without you working too hard. The secret code should weed out most bad applications so you are only reading the good ones. The phone screen should eliminate any weird interviews where you waste an hour with someone you know you won't hire after a minute. And the Written Project, well that should weed out candidates that are not going to be compatible with your work style. With all these levels of screening – most of which require little or no time from you, there is likely to be only one candidate standing by the time you get to the interview. The interview is a final gut check for you and a chance for you to show off and chase the candidate for a change. Take a minute and think through the next job you will fill in your organization:

1. Do you have a written project in mind for that role (If not, create one now.)
2. Are you prepared to lean back and let a candidate chase you until you are absolutely sure they are the right fit for your organization? (If not, what inner work needs to happen?)
3. If you have a Rockstar soulmate employee in front of you, will you be

prepared to chase them when the time is right and make sure working in your organization will serve them? (If not, what would give you that clarity and confidence?)

CHAPTER 8

Incubating Intrinsic Motivation

Compensation always felt fucked up to me as an employee. It always felt like there was no rhyme or reason for the decisions that were made by management. Now that I'm the one running the show, I can see how completely right that assessment probably was!

As much as this book serves as a tool for building an amazing team, it also serves as a bitch session about all the shitty bosses, in all the shitty companies, with all the shitty comp plans I ever worked at. After 20 years as a poorly and confusingly-compensated employee, I was mad as hell and not willing to take it anymore, so I started a company where, in short order, I became the person compensating people for the work in a totally fucked-up way.

It turns out creating great comp plans is really hard and confusing. This is because, in large measure, companies don't start off with a strategy and backing into one can feel nearly impossible after the horse has left the barn. I know, because at The Author Incubator I've had to do this and I can tell you the only thing worse than fixing your comp plan is going to bed knowing some people make more money than others for no good reason.

When I was an employee, it seemed like there was a secret code to how salary was determined. It had something to do with how well you negotiated your opening salary and how good your timing was when asking for raises. And let me be clear, I was often the highest compensated person in any role I ever took because I'm fantastic at both, but that certainly was not what made me the most deserving employee. Salary negotiation and asking for raises seem like simple skills we could teach everyone, and, okay, they probably are, but having a fair and logical system is so much better! Instead of putting the onus on the employee, put it where it should be, which is, in my opinion, on the employer.

While I don't believe conscious bias has anything to do with compensation, I think there is a combination of unconscious bias and priority logic that leads to women and people of color being comped at lower rates. And the statistics back that up. The problem is we are blaming the employers without addressing the right problem. The problem we address is bias, but teaching people about unconscious bias or teaching women to be better negotiators does not solve this problem. Because the problem is really about having an organized and thought-through system about how employees are compensated BEFORE you even meet them and know their color or gender.

The first crazy thing I am going to tell you – and you aren't going to like it – is that you have to make your employee salaries public. Daniel Indiviglio wrote about this convincingly in his 2011 article in The Atlantic entitled "The Case for Making Wages Public: Better Pay, Better Workers" I know this can seem impossible and like it's going to cause so much swirl, but think about it. In the government, salaries are public. There is a chart of the pay scale and when a job is posted it says what the salary grade and step is for that position.

Salary Bands

Even if you don't want to disclose your full salaries you can create a simple salary band or range system. This way, starting now, (even if you have employees who fall outside of this band) when you are negotiating salaries for roles, you know you can't take new people if their starting salary is above the band limits. Ideally you want someone to start between the bottom and the middle of a band so there is room for growth without a promotion.

Here's what our salary bands look like at The Author Incubator.

Entry Level: This is someone who is executing very specific tasks that are given to them. They are not paid to think, strategize, solve problems, or even manage their schedule. They are paid to take some pressure off their boss and handle specific, regular tasks, like reporting, answering emails or phones, or doing short-term administrative projects so that the person they report to can be more productive at the higher-level thinking tasks. These employees have titles like Coordinator, Assistant, and Analyst. The salary band here in Washington, DC, in 2020 is $30K to $49K.

Junior Management: The difference between entry level and management at our company is something we call ownership. If you are a MANAGER, you are expected to own the responsibilities of your job regardless of the time it takes to get it done or the hoops you have to jump through. No one is coming to save you. If you are managing these tasks, their completion is on you without excuses. Management means responsibility. Many of our managers have direct reports, but not all. These positions have titles that include the word manager – like our Marketing Manager and our Managing Editors. These are comped at $50K to $69K and make up the large band with about 50% of the bell curve in this spot.

Mid-level Management: The only difference between junior management and mid-level management, or directors, is cross-team responsibilities. As a manager you need to take full-responsibility for your work, and, if you have direct reports, their work. But as a director you also have to take responsibility for the way your team's work affects OTHER teams. Directors have to be more efficient at their management jobs because they need 50% of their time to communicate what is happening between and among teams. This level of management is critical to your company's success and the hardest to build and nurture. We have two levels of mid-level management. Stage one is our director level, with a salary band of $70 to 89K, and stage two is our senior director level, with a salary band of $90K to $109K.

Senior Management: Senior managers need emotional and intellectual capacity far beyond your mid-level managements. The difference between mid-level management and senior management is, frankly, the ability to speak the CEOs language, to manage the timing, to do the tasks, and to get the intangibles. If a mid-level manager can manage up to 8 people, senior management caps out at around 650 people in a small company. They can manage 8 people, who each manage 8 people who each manage 8 people. This is because senior managers don't confuse the value of their TIME with the value of their LEVERAGE. At our small business, we band senior management base salaries from $110K to $160K.

Any earnings over $160K in our company come from bonuses, commissions, and distributions.

Performance Bonuses

Once your salaries are sorted, there is still a major issue, which is bonus-based compensation plans. In addition to salaries, there will be reasons you want to pay employees more for performance. My first rule here is that a salary is provided in exchange for doing the job. So when it comes to anything above that salary plus a moderate 1% to 5% annual raise, the salary is what the salary is. As the business owner, or business unit manager, you have to constantly remind yourself everyone is replaceable. If it's not a win-win for your employee and you, you should quickly let that employee go and put someone else in the role to do the tasks. Some CEOs try to use performance-based compensation to keep employees or bribe them to want something different than what they want. This will backfire. Your job as the manager is to find out what the employee actually wants and, if the job is in alignment with those wants, pay them a salary. Don't make their business your business.

I used to use bonuses to try to bribe my team into behavior that wasn't natural to them. I offered the entire team a bonus based on monthly and quarterly sales numbers, even for employees not directly connected to the sales job. I wanted everyone on the team to be looking for opportunities to close sales, since that would mean a bigger bonus for them. About halfway through the year there was a big sales project which about a third of the team was involved with. If the project went well it would mean the different between an 8% bonus and a 12% bonus. Even for the lowest-paid employee this would be a couple grand. Surely, with thousands of dollars on the line, I thought, they will make sure this projected is completed flawlessly. Nope. Nope. And nope again.

What I came to discover is that one of my gifts as CEO, and one you or any business leader can develop, is to hold a bigger vision and a bigger list of tasks in your head than the average employee. Most employees, even when incentivized by bonuses, can't make the connections between how their work today might affect those bonuses set to happen weeks or months in the future that they heard about weeks or months in the past. Even money – money they really would like to have – doesn't improve performance.

Teresa Amabile calls this the "Intrinsic Motivation Principle" in her article "How to Kill Creativity" (Harvard Business Review, September - October 1998): "People will be most creative when they feel motivated primarily by the interest, satisfaction, and challenge of the work itself – not by external pressures."

In his TED talk, author Dan Pink reached exactly the same conclusion about the problems of extrinsic motivation, recommending instead "an approach built much more around intrinsic motivation, around the desire to do things because they matter, because we like it, because they're interesting, because they're part of something important."

Dr. Bernd Irlenbusch of the London School of Economics takes it a step further, saying, "financial incentives can result in a negative impact on overall performance."

In short, a bonus is a trap.

At The Author Incubator, we do pay bonuses, but in an unusual way. We use the concept of the

Net Promoter Score or NPS for every employee. NPS is a management tool that can be used to gauge customer satisfaction, but we use it to gauge employee success. The Net Promoter Score is calculated based on responses to a single question: "How likely is it that you would recommend our company/product/service to a friend or colleague?" The scoring for this answer is most often based on a 0 to 10 scale. At our company every team member is asked once a quarter to rate their peers by answering just this question: "How likely are you to recommend a family member or colleague to work with this person?"

Everyone in the company gets a score from 1 to 10, averaging all their NPS ratings from coworkers. I always found good coworkers to be the best reason to stay at a job and bad ones the best reason to leave. With this totally blind system, anyone who is scoring below an average of 7 is not a super awesome colleague and is likely to be moved out of the company or the role. How awesome would it be to work at a company where you rated all of your co-workers a 10?

Of all the scores given by our team, 78% are scores of a 10 and only 1.2% of all scores are under a 7. As a culture creator, this lets me know we have a team of people who love their co-workers, but it also gives me a way to provide a performance-based bonuses tied to more intrinsic motivation. Employees are welcome to opt out of the bonus plan if they don't want to rate or be rated. If participating they get a score and that single score is the basis for their annual bonus as decided by their peers. So a score of 9.2 would give you a 9.2% bonus. Say you earn $50,000 total (before taxes and other withholdings) in 2019 and your average score is 9.2 – then your bonus will be $50,000 x 9.2% = $4,600.

The lowest score you could get is a 1 (a 1% bonus), but this would be hard to get. Every single team member would have to rate you a 1 and you would still have to be keeping your job. This seems very unlikely to me and has never happened. In fact, we haven't seen an NPS below 8.

This means bonuses of at least 7% (probably 8%) are inevitable, which means the level of confidence that bonuses will get paid and can be estimated increases confidence around compensation and intrinsic satisfaction.

Commissions

There is one area where performance compensation can work and that is with your direct sales force. In a perfect team the sales force should be paid a salary on par with the senior management of the company. Sales is a hard job that requires a unique skill set and personality and the ability to handle a lot of pressure. Your sales people should be among the highest paid in your company.

I've worked in many companies where that was the case, but the compensation for sales was commission only. In the early days of my company I tried that approach but I found it very difficult to really get the sales teams full time and attention with the commission-only structure. Commission-only sales people come to understand opportunity cost extremely well. If it doesn't look like sales are easily closing they will let their attention wander quickly and with little recourse. As a business person you want a commitment from sales to figure things out when shit is not closing or when the sales process is longer or harder than it should be.

I realized a commission-only sales structure was really me hedging my bets to minimize my risk while expecting the sales person to take all the risk and go all-in on me. I like having the leverage commissions allow to encourage the behavior I want, especially at the end of the month. I recommend 50-75% of comp for sales come from salary and 25-50% from bonuses. That way you have enough money to play with the incentive for hitting end of month and end of quarter goals, but not so much of the total compensation that you don't have the employees' full and unfettered attention.

High-Potential Employees (HiPots)

Nowhere is attention more important than with the 15-20% of your team who are high-potential employees. A HiPot is someone for whom career and career growth is a top priority. They do not separate work from fun, because kicking ass at work is a HiPot's favorite thing to do. Family and hobbies are great, but career success is what lights up a HiPot. A HiPot sees success as increasing responsibility commensurate with increasing pay. A HiPot wants the opportunity to do their best a work and be rewarded for it quickly.

Most employees don't have the HiPot edge, and that is great. You want 80% of your workforce to be folks who want a job that is aligned with their personal values and morals. This is an employee who believes in the company, lives the values, wants a job to provide fulfillment and money but in a limited way. Standard employees want to limit work to 40 hours a week and focus on family and other hobbies as well as work.

Rule number one is to quickly identify your HiPots. It might change over time, but these are your company unicorns and you won't be able to grow without being able to catch 'em and curate 'em. Don't be mad at standard employees for not fitting the HiPot mold. And don't be delusional about ambitious team members who lack the other half of the HiPot equation – talent. Not only does a HiPot have to want it, but they have to be good enough to go get it. There are another 5% of employees who are standard employees who think they are HiPots but they just don't have that "thing" that would truly qualify them as having high potential.

You will know within 90 days if you have a HiPot. You'll know because they will be in early, done late, asking questions on the weekend, and generally blowing your mind by learning their job in half the time of most people and then getting things banged out that have been on the to-do list for months.

Structuring Raises

When you identify a HiPot, give them a massive 10% raise in the first 90 days and let them know they are a HiPot. See if they agree with your assessment and plan out their goals for the next 2-5 years. You should be able to list in advance the date for every single raise and promotion. Here's how that looked for one of our employees:

$40K – June 2017 – Assistant

$60K – September 2017 – Manager

$70K – March 2018 – Director

$85K – April 2018 – Senior Director

$100K – September 2018 – VP

$110K – March 2019 – no title change

$120K – September 2019 – C-level title TBD

$140K – Jan 2020 – President

$160K – Jan 2021 – CEO

This was, obviously, a 4-year plan from the mail room to the corner office. Not every HiPot will have this exact journey, but to keep a HiPot they really have to see a 50-100% increase in their salary every year or you will lose their attention.

Most people will not have the capacity for the emotional growth and pressure that this requires, which is why standard employees will make up the majority of your workforce. Standard employees should still get a map of the career they can expect for the next 3-5 years so they can plan and set expectations accordingly. The career map will show them raises and titles for the next 3-5 years and might look like this:

$60K – June 2017 – Managing Editor

$62K – June 2018 – Managing Editor

$64K – June 2019 – Managing Editor

$66K – June 2020 – Managing Editor

$68K – June 2021 – Managing Editor

$70K – June 2022 – Senior Managing Editor

In addition to their salary and the bonus and/or commission components discussed above, standard employees should get a 1-5% cost of living adjustment. You can properly set this by checking with the US Bureau of Labor & Statistics to get the annual inflation rate. For the past few years it's been around 2%. The 2017 inflation rate was 2.13%. The inflation rate in 2018 was 2.44%. At the time of writing we are on track in 2019 for an inflation rate of about 1.9%. In order to keep someone's salary the same, you have to give them an annual raise that matches the annual inflation rate. This percentage is the one I would use for all the of B players you want to keep. A 2% raise, or a raise that matches annual inflation, basically says, "You are doing your job well. And you aren't freaking us out, so no need to be freaked out yourself."

An annual raise BELOW the annual inflation rate (or no raise at all) is basically a way of telling an employee they should be looking for another job and the end is near. Anyone on a performance improvement plan should not get a raise. In fact, set a policy that annual raises are delayed until 3 months after the completion of any performance improvement plans in progress. Otherwise, it sends confusing mixed messages. Now if you give an annual raise over the inflation rate you are giving a gold star. I recommend a raise of 3-5% (or whatever twice the annual inflation rate is) for your most valuable players, including all HiPots and all standard employees who are kicking ass and getting their jobs done efficiently.

There is one more type of raise you want to have in your back pocket to motivate both standard and HiPot employees and that's an Above & Beyond raise. This is a raise of 5-10% to recognize when an employee is going above and beyond their job description and you want to recognize it in a big way. This shouldn't be taken as standard practice and must be reserved for special occasions. I use this type of raise when I "miss" recognizing a HiPot by their 90-day mark. Sometimes you have an amazing employee who just didn't shine in those first 90 days. When you see it, you have to reward it with a 10% raise and by moving that employee onto the HiPot ladder. I've also used the Above & Beyond raise when I have a standard employee who isn't in a position for a promotion or a significant raise but who regularly does things outside of their job description and with excellence and no excuses. This can be comped with a bonus or a raise, but of course a raise has longer-term positive effects for the employee because their cost of living adjustments will now be based on this higher number. A raise is also helpful to the company if you are in a cash flow jam or want to limit cash outlay.

Benefits

In addition to salary, other benefits do matter. I have found it hard to recruit for candidates in the United States without offering Health Insurance. It's not entirely logical but it is a marketplace expectation and it's worth just figuring out. We also offer a 401K and disability and life insurance but those never affected recruiting like health care does. These are table stakes and I don't have much that is clever to add, but where I have spent considerable time is on the issue of paid time off (PTO) and other forms of leave.

When I first started my business, I was a fan of the Netflix approach to PTO – take as much as you want, just get the job done. This seemed ENTIRELY reasonable and it's what I was doing as the CEO after all. It felt hypocritical to expect anything else.

And then there was the summer of 2018 when just about everyone in the company decided to take the entire month of August off (including me btw). Sales crashed, client experience was in the shitter, we almost lost the company that summer while everyone was "getting the job done" according to their own definition. Clearly Netflix has better implementation of their policy than I do. I told everyone to manage their time, but I meant, please manage it to my expectations and while we are at it, could you read my mind?

I may have mentioned, communication is impossible.

"Get the job done" means too many things to too many people and for me, the all you can eat PTO plan really did not work.

In 2019 we switched to a new approach where everyone got 4 weeks of vacation time but it was distributed as 5 business days per quarter, use it or lose it. What I like about this plan is that vacation time is much more spaced out and I don't have to police people's definitions of getting the job done. This way, worst case, they are out of the office for a week and we can pick up the ball when they get back.

Step 5 Conclusion: Align the Compensation

The problem with most compensation plans, especially for small businesses, is that they're not thought out and don't have a set of rules around them. This makes your best employees do way too much math trying to ascertain if they are getting what's fair. By having transparent salaries or salary bands, plus transparent rules on how raises and bonuses are given, and by saying who makes the rules and how they are made, you eliminate a lot of unnecessary and time-consuming speculation. You will likely avoid the drama. People have a lot of drama over their salaries but there is math and there is drama. In this case, the math is simple if you have a clearly designed comp plan. "At our company here's how we do it, I totally get if that doesn't work for you." This lets your employees keep their own drama instead of dragging other employees into it.

1. Before you go announcing anything, do an audit of what you pay people and notice the lack of rhyme or reason. You are going to have to sort this out. You might lose

people in the process or pay some folx more. It will be worth it to make 'em beg to work for you.

2. Start by creating salary bands and for a year hire within those bands. See if anyone outside the bands just ages out of the system and moves on.
3. If you still have people outside the bands before you make the salaries public, prepare to have some difficult and transparent conversations. You will want to release your salaries as well as your system for raises and other compensation metrics so people how what to expect.

This whole book is about making them beg to work for you. If you want that – employees beating a path to your door even in a tight labor market – well, then you have to have fair and well thought through compensation policies. Part of an employer's job is to provide financial safety and stability, and you can't do that with an ad-hoc, unconscious, bias-driven plan for employee compensation.

CHAPTER 9

Slow Is Smooth. Smooth Is Fast

It's one thing to find great employees who can't wait to be a part of your mission; it's another to get them on board in their roles, making a difference, and contributing to the bottom line. The reason I think it's so important to "make 'em beg to work for you" is because the energy of having an employee who truly feels like getting this job is a dream come true for them is a focus game-changer. It aligns your mutual desires for the employee to be successful in the role. It changes you from natural adversaries (the traditional union model – workers' rights need to be protected) to natural allies (we both get our needs met by you doing what needs to be done).

When you "make 'em beg to work for you," what they are begging for is the chance to more quickly accomplish their own personal goals – maybe it's buying a house, losing 50 lbs., creating a life where they spend 4 months of the year out of the country, or becoming CEO before they turn 40. When you can map your employees' personal goals with the job it's a true win-win.

That mutual victory requires an effective onboarding process, and I'd say here is where most companies fall flat. I've had 7 corporate jobs in my career and not one of them had a real onboarding process. In every case, I spent the first week or so drinking from a fire hose, absorbing all the information I could, taking on tasks as assigned, and asking questions as I went. Then, after a few weeks of that, I began inventing my own ways to meet what I understood the objectives to be. It was frustrating and inefficient for me and, I'm sure now, for my boss. The alternative, which I'm going to teach you here, can seem slow and frustrating at the beginning, but in the end will be fast and efficient and save you from having to replace as many employees that didn't work out.

As they say in the military, "Slow is smooth and smooth is fast."

Hire Before You Need 'Em

Crushing blow coming up.... You are probably hiring too late.

To "make 'em beg to work for you," you have to hire your employees about 90 days before you need them. The salary you pay an employee for the first 3 months is their training budget. You are going to invest for 3 months before expecting any returns. (Note, if you find a HiPot you will likely get a return on your investment sooner than 90 days, which is why you will give them a big, juicy raise at their 90-day anniversary, but this will only happen 15 - 20% of the time. More on this in the previous chapter on raises.)

You need to be able to forecast when you will need employees so you can hire them 3 months in advance. This is a topic for another book, but if you don't know how to do this, I recommend reading Pam Prior's book, *Your First CFO* as a starting point. Without having her as my first CFO, I don't think I would have learned how to project when I would need an employee so I could begin hiring at the right times to create the kind of company culture people would really want to be a part of.

Everything I teach here can be adapted if you are under more time pressure, but what I'm about to teach is the ideal scenario if you do have a proper training period. The problem with the fire hose approach is it leads to a stressed employee who basically assumes all the responsibilities without actually knowing how to do them and so the tasks are done poorly and with lots of errors and mistakes for about a year, until the employee begins to understand what they are doing and how everything is connected, and then they start completely recreating the role and all the tasks. What I recommend instead is focusing on mastery of one task at a time. Instead of the fire hose approach, slow way, way down and start spoon-feeding very limited information to your new employee so real understanding can be achieved before you rely on that person for execution.

One of my authors, Angela Kelly Robeck, is a teacher and she was helping me with this from a classroom perspective. In order to help a class understand a concept, Angela explained, the process is: First I teach you, then I do it and you watch, then I do it and you help, then you do it and I help, and finally you do it and I watch. That means a task needs to be done WITH the employee 4 times before they are on their own with the task. Compare that to the old model which I came up under, which was: I explain it while not doing it, you take notes and hope you get it right in a few weeks when the task comes up. What the what? No wonder so many employees produce work that feels disappointing. More is required of you if you want folx to beg to come work for you.

The First 90 Days

Here's a sample onboarding example you can use as a template for bringing your next employee onto your team. Start with a list of all the tasks you will need to teach. The job description can be a good place to start for that. Then break them up into 3 months so that each month they are learning a third of their job. Then schedule time on the calendar to do each of these tasks with the employee. While a job description might have 10 or 15 bullet points, a management onboarding plan will have many more because one task, like "manage events," might have 20 or 30 micro skills that need to be taught. This onboarding plan is for our Client Success Specialist role.

June Activities – By the end of June, employee will:

1. Be setting up Basecamp for all new clients
2. Do password resets for Basecamp/Kajabi
3. Know how to track assignments and manage milestones in Basecamp – even if Mila is still doing it

4. Keep cohort list up to date in FB
5. Have a list of frequently asked questions in the FB group
6. Watch all training videos for 9-week virtual and live events, including doing all assignments except writing an actual manuscript
7. Create new member orientation and present it and record it to a test client

July Activity – By the end of July, employee will: (June skills in italics)

8. Set up Basecamp for all new clients
9. Do password resets for Basecamp/Kajabi
10. Check in all assignments for all active clients; manage and adjust milestones to make sure all authors hit the final deadline
11. Keep cohort list up to date in FB
12. Answer all customer service questions for authors in transformation
13. Do new member orientations one-on-one for each new client added in July; record all.

14. Know how to create travel packets and get hotel codes
15. Have a plan for taking questions before Angela's Tuesday calls
16. Start running Thursday calls as deadline check-ins
17. Know how to mail welcome gifts to authors-in-transform.
18. Introduce Angela on one call.

August Activity – By the end of August, employee will: (June & July skills in italics)

19. Set up Basecamp for all new clients
20. Do password resets for Basecamp/Kajabi
21. Check in all assignments for all active clients; manage and adjust milestones to make sure all authors hit the final deadline
22. Keep cohort list up to date in FB
23. Answer all customer service questions for authors in transformation
24. Do new member orientations one-on-one
25. Create travel packets and get hotel codes

26. Mail welcome gifts to authors-in-transform.
27. Take questions before Angela's Tuesday calls
28. Run Thursday calls as deadline check-ins
29. Introduce Angela on Tuesday calls
30. Test weekly GROUP orientation
31. Observe/assist at your first The Author's Way Live – organize gifts for hotel, approve room set up, introduce Angela, run the breaks, take pictures at event

September Activity – By the end of September (and ongoing) employee will:

32. Set up Basecamp for all new clients
33. Do password resets for Basecamp/Kajabi
34. Check in all assignments for all active clients; manage and adjust milestones to make sure all authors hit the final deadline
35. Keep cohort list up to date in FB
36. Answer all customer service questions for authors in transformation

37. Do new member orientations one-on-one or in group
38. Create travel packets and get hotel codes
39. Mail welcome gifts to authors-in-transform.
40. Take questions before Angela's Tuesday calls
41. Run Thursday calls as deadline check-ins
42. Introduce Angela on Tuesday calls
43. Co-host The Author's Way Live – organize gifts for hotel, approve room set up, introduce Angela, run the breaks, take pictures at event

Less Than You Think, But Better

The bad news is, one employee, even properly onboarded, can probably handle a lot less than you think they should be able to. The good news is, if you give them a lot less, there is a very good chance they will do it a lot better and have much more happiness in the process. In fact, at the end of the day, each role should probably have 5 big bullet points that measure their ultimate success and whether they are an A player on the team.

I've come to find that, for most employees, having more than 5 big goals or rocks in their head at once leads to shame and blame. They literally can't handle it, which causes anger, embarrassment, and finger-pointing. It's so much better to have happy employees taking on less and doing it well. For each of our roles we have 3 - 5 bullet points of what success in that role looks like. We call it our "Babies Die List."

Morbid, I know. But here's how it works: For most things you do in any role, how you do them and when you do them won't make the difference between success or failure, and so I find myself saying, "That's cool. It's not like babies are going to die if we do it that way." But there are some things where "babies" do in fact die. These are the most critical, non-negotiable, ultimate results that matter most. They are our "babies," and each employee has 3 - 5 "babies" they must tend to.

One of our company's 3 core values is "Results Matter Most" – not how long it takes, not how hard you work, not what celebrities share what you did in social media – nope! None of that! What matters most are the results. For no babies to die these are the 3 - 5 things you have to find a way, come hell or high water, to make happen.

Here are the Babies Die Lists for 2 roles in our company, the Client Success Specialist and the Publishing Manager.

Ultimate Results that Determine Success as Client Success Specialist (in order of importance)

1. All authors turn in assembled manuscript by due date
2. All authors onboarded efficiently (within 24 hours – Basecamp set up, cohort list updated, welcome gifts/travel pack mailed, orientation scheduled)
3. All customer service, including password resets, within 24 hours (ideally within an hour)

4. Angela gets on and off weekly calls within 2 hours.
5. Takes ownership for client services for The Author's Way

<u>Ultimate Results that Determine Success as Publishing Manager (in order of importance)</u>

1. Authors must have eBook live on Red Carpet Day
2. Authors must make self-publish or traditionally publish decision within 30 days
3. Authors self-publishing or traditional publishing with Difference Press must have their digital print proof within 90 days of decision (within 120 days of Red Carpet Launch).
4. Authors going with traditional must transfer smoothly
5. Authors must get the royalties we owe them in the time we promised

The cool thing about the Babies Die List is that it gives total and complete accountability for these items to one person in the organization and takes their boss (and their boss's boss) out of the loop on these things unless there is a problem. This is how we develop leaders who love their jobs instead of minions waiting for tasks.

When you have people begging to work for you, it's easy to find people who can own their area of responsibility and who are fully empowered, responsible, and accountable for their areas of success. This is how you get a team filled with people who are better than you at the things they do.

Once an employee is on board with the culture, mission, and vision of the company, and they see how, beyond the paycheck, this job is going to get them other things they want in their life, then, with a slow, smooth onboarding process they can be given the guidance and direction they need to make the decisions for their "babies" themselves. Total and complete ownership.

I know some people like the idea of a self-managing company. I haven't found the way to make that really work, but this approach, where you find the right person, onboard them slowly and carefully, and give them a very limited set of things they have total, complete responsibility for, is pretty close to self-managing.

Hiring leaders, hiring your future managers, hiring the people who will form your leadership team is so much different than hiring a group of people who are just transactionally performing tasks.

My dad used to say to his employees, "I don't pay you to think." You can go that way, but not if you want to scale out of 7 figures with sanity. Yes, your employees do need to get things done, but they also need to be strategic thinkers. They need to be able to drive strategic execution. And they need to be better than you at a smaller scope of activity, so that they can get better results than you.

Step 6 Conclusion: Nurture the Talent

Hiring isn't the end of the journey to having a highly talented and committed team. Being an awesome company and having a smart and focused person who wants to work for you are two awesome and important parts of the equation, but you can't just expect a new employee to jump in an add value. Integrating the new employee protects the investment you paid in hiring them.

1. Make sure you are not hiring when your need is desperate.
2. Identify the 3-5 most critical responsibilities for the role - the "babies will die" jobs
3. Break down the steps to being able to be fully responsible for those 3-5 critical tasks over the course of 90 days. If the onboarding goes well and they take full ownership of their responsibilities within 90 days, they get a raise!

Of course it's also possible the 90 days doesn't go well. In that case there are 2 options. Repeat the 90 days (with no raise of course), or let the employee go with love. In our last step we will talk about yielding the reality of the fit.

CHAPTER 10

Letting Go

It's always chaotic at the Disney World ticket counter right when the park is opening. They open the park an hour earlier for guests of the hotels on the property, but I was staying with my 4-year-old at my dad's place and had driven in for his first taste of the Mouse. It was a special Mom & Me day and I didn't mind the lines at all – holding hands with my big boy and knowing on the other side we'd rent a stroller so I could put my heavy purse/mom bag down.

My Blackberry rang and I had nothing else to do so I picked it up. It was my boss: "Hey, Angela, Great news! We are going to be able to keep you on as a contractor." It was a confusing morning anyway, but this made no sense. I was the chief marketing officer for a software company. I was in the middle of writing our latest book on Windows Server Backup. We were processing 1900 leads a month with our inside sales team. I'd just gotten my 2010 plan passed. What. Was. Happening?

"We've decided to switch to a new strategy focusing on resellers more and lead gen less, so the fit just isn't there, but we've got a couple months of consulting dollars for you."

It was just after 9 am. It was about to be one of the most expensive days of my life. And. I. Was. Fired?

My brain could barely process what was happening. I'd been fired before, but never starting with the words "Great news!" and never so out of left field. We did Disney World, and I have the Buzz and Woody pictures to prove it, but as I walked through the park that day I promised myself I would never again be in a position to get fired. The feeling of being sideswiped and sucker-punched at the same time seemed more than I could handle. I handled it, of course, in my usual way, with carbs and sugar, but something changed in me.

An Object in Motion

My plan at The Author Incubator was to only hire awesome people and never have to fire anyone. This is the problem with the bus metaphor. If your business was a bus, then you could just find the coolest people and put them in the right seats. But your business is not a bus; it's more like the rotating cast of a Broadway Musical with contracts ending and starting and swings getting promoted, and illnesses and injuries. Your needs shift as different actors come on the stage or another musical starts or ends changing the available cast members for your show. There are so many variables that I couldn't see as an employee. And things change on the employee side too. Sometimes someone who was super focused has a change at home and can't seem to keep their eye on the ball. People are not fixed in time.

Some people will be a fit for a while and then not anymore, either for their reasons or the company's reasons. I stopped thinking about getting our team structure right and started thinking about it as a moving, living, changing, flowing superorganism. When I write down my org chart it's like surfing the waves. I can see a wave coming and think about how I want it to go or how it could go and the org chart becomes a way of journaling or capturing that thought. But it's not "done" and it's never going to be done.

If you are waiting to make a couple hires and be done growing, let me dispel that notion right now. If you start to think of your team more like a professional sports team you will see how you need to keep bringing in players and moving players out. This is a much healthier perspective for everyone. When we are in the cast for the show we are as close as family, but NOT family. We are aware we could get a better role and leave the cast, or be injured and replaced, but if and when that happens we will still likely have an allegiance to this show and these actors in it wherever they end up. We will always say "We were in a show together once!" but we will not be family forever. And that's okay. We were in a Company together that that's enough!

No Sudden Moves

After what happen with me at Disney World, I decided I wanted to create a company where you would not be surprised when it was your time to go. The thing in sports is that there are games. You can tell if you are playing and you can tell if you are playing well. It's easy to get a sense of what is happening and whether you are going to be released or traded. I felt like, for me, that was less obvious and I wanted to make it more obvious.

From the beginning I tell my team, "If things are not working out, I'm going to let you know long before we would get to the point of firing you." The truth is, recruiting and training employees are expensive and we only hire rock stars, so it's in everyone's best interest to try to change the role or the requirements of the job so that it's a win-win. If it's not a win-win – meaning if the organization and the employee aren't equally benefiting from the situation – the parties should agree to move on, but it's essential to give that time to shake and bake.

I know the general advice is to hire slow and fire fast. My advice is to hire fast and fire slow. I know! I know! It's annoying, right? But here is my take.

When you know, you know. If you set up elaborate hoops like the ones I described in the interviewing chapter, you will intuitively know if the person is a fit. If they jump through every hoop (which is the only way to get through) and you aren't begging them to work for you as much as they are begging to work for you, then it's a no! You have to be quickly and energetically leaping out of your chair. From the second you post an ad until you have someone hired should be no more than one week. Often you can post an ad and have a "hell yes" candidate in just a day or two. You will feel the energy.

But when it comes to saying goodbye, I feel like there is a human side to it – on both sides. I don't think people should quit quickly and I don't think we should fire them quickly. This is an actual human with financial responsibilities and identity-related issues, on one side – and on the other side, this is an organization with coworkers you will be messing with and clients who might get hurt by you leaving. Now we are a team; we are connected; we are a part of the same organism. To just quit or to fire someone with no process to it feels cold and misguided.

Instead, what I recommend is at the very first sign something is off – and I mean the very first teeny tiny sign, say something. It's important for employees to know things are fluid. The patriarchy tells us things are fixed, but it's a lie. The idea of a fixed truth is a concept based in the masculine. Black and white. Yes or no. On or off. These binary structures served our organizations well Post-Industrial Revolution, but these systems are falling apart. You are not the master and your employee is not the slave. The divine feminine represents the connection to the part of your consciousness responsible for nurturing, intuition, and empathy, regardless of your gender. As the divine feminine rises in the collective consciousness these traits are more important when businesses and employees decide if it's time to stay or go.

This is all very esoteric but what it boils down to is that you should trust your intuition as an employer and employee and use your voice. In the old paradigm being unhappy meant stuffing your feelings and living with a job or a worker you hated, or exploding with a Trumpian "You're fired." Or an equally definitive, "Take this job and shove it."

There is so much in the middle to be explored. Here are the steps I recommend the minute you are unhappy with an employee, even if it's their first day of work:

1. Tell the employee you are always going to be forthcoming when something isn't working

2. Tell them what isn't working for you
3. Ask them to work with you to find a creative way around this

Our job is to work together to keep the win-win front and center. "Here's what you want" (3 years of experience before you go to grad school). "Here's what I want" (someone to edit 60 books a year for me). Great – we both have a stake in this and there is lots of negotiating room where we BOTH get what we want. But we must lean into the fact this is going to require ongoing nurturing. We aren't going to have the baby and then drop it on the floor and let it raise itself.

The Difference Between Nurturing and Dragging It Out

I knew pretty early on things weren't working with Amanda. I desperately wanted them to work. And that was one of the biggest problems. Amanda was an old friend from high school and she came on to do a multi-tasking heavy role which required a lot of judgment calls. She didn't seem to be very good at making them. It was only a couple weeks in when we had the "How do we make this a win-win?" chat. I could tell Amanda was stuck in the master/slave dialectic. She wasn't pushing back on me at all. If I'd told her she needed to walk exclusively on her hands, in that meeting she would have told me she would give it a try.

The meeting went fine and we had some action items but I could feel she was afraid of losing her job and wanted to do whatever to keep it. This will not work and will not create a win-win.

A few weeks later I tried again. This time I asked her what she wanted. She had some personal goals: to find a relationship and to find her passion. She felt like the job was something she COULD do, but it wasn't her thing. But... she didn't know what her thing was.

As the weeks passed, more balls got dropped. It was clear I couldn't keep Amanda in that role. But it was equally clear she didn't want to go. I met with her again and explained the lack of a win-win and asked her for a plan to fix it. "We tried my plan and it didn't work. Now let's try yours. I don't want to say goodbye. I want to make this work. You tell me how it can be a win-win. Find any job in the company, anything you think you can do to solve a problem for me, and then tell me how that job will help you solve your problem. The only requirement for my request is that you don't present a plan that says, 'Let's keep doing what we've been doing. I'll try harder to be happier and better at it.'"

I gave her a week, I think, to put the plan together. The day we were supposed to meet, the meeting kept getting pushed. I felt like, energetically, she didn't want to have the meeting. It finally happened at 6 pm. We were both exhausted, but I tried to perk myself up and be present. I planted my feet on the floor. Even though my feet were in shoes, I spread my toes as wide as I could and pictured tentacles coming from the bottom of each toe going to the core of the earth, sending the energy of the earth up through my legs.

"You're on!" I told her.

And Amanda presented the plan. She walked me through all of her thinking and journaling for the week. She rattled off how we'd gotten to that moment. She told me how much she loved me and the company (the feeling was mutual) and then she said her plan was to keep doing what she's been doing but try harder and be happier and better at it – but what she really wanted was to write and maybe someday she could make that happen but since she wasn't qualified to be a writer this would have to do for now.

That was NOT a win-win.

I knew it was my responsibility in that moment to terminate her employment. The goddess whispered in my ear. The termination letter had been created and was in my top drawer as we spoke. And yet, my lips did not move in that direction.

"I don't get it," I said. "This is what I told you NOT to come back with."

She didn't argue. "I know," she said. "But I really don't want to leave this job."

It was probably me being selfish, not wanting to do recruiting, not wanting to be the one who had to fire her. I don't know why but I told her we would try it for another 30 days. On day 29 I was wondering what I was going to do. Burying my head in the sand seemed like a reasonable option. (Adulting is hard.) And then the phone call came. While driving to work Amanda had been in a major car accident. She was in a coma. No telling if she'd make it or if she could ever work again.

Now I KNOW I didn't cause that accident. I am not delusional. But I do think if I had been brave enough to terminate her employment when I knew I should have, she would not have been in the car that day on her way to work. That accident would not have happened.

The universe WILL get your attention when you are out of alignment. Mark my words. There is no way to hide. I knew we were both out of alignment in that relationship, but I wanted to find a way to pull it back to center. That is not always our job.

It's like a marriage. Some marriages are just not meant to be saved, and neither are some jobs. Yes, you should try a couple things over a couple months to see if you can find the win-win, but if it's not there, you have to have the discernment to say goodbye, even if, in the moment, the employee might hate you for it.

The purpose of letting someone go is to help them come into a deeper communion with where they are supposed to be.

Step 7 Conclusion: Yield with Love

Saying goodbye is never easy but it can be the right thing. Not every business relationship is going to be the perfect fit. People come into your business for a reason, a season, or the whole journey but you never know which when you hire them. Trust your instincts when you hire. Nurture their integration into the company, and then be honest if it isn't working.

1. Hire fast. Trust your instinct and trust that you will know what to do if it doesn't go how you expected.

2. Fire slow. Yes, I know it's expensive, but being an asshole will always be more expensive. Look for a win-win. Try different roles if you are both willing. Be open to the container looking different than expects.
3. Always yield to love. If you have given it a few tries and it's still not coming together, find a way to part with love. If it's not a win-win for you both, then it's not a fit.

Love is the only strategy here. See your employee as a whole human and encourage they do the same for you. Everyone wants to be seen, recognized, challenged, and respected. Do that even if it's not a fit for this person to star in your show.

CHAPTER 11

The Prize Never Chases

The problem with building a great team is that it's nothing like building a great house. Building a great team is an ongoing process. I would say the key ingredient is being a great company. If you are in integrity, clear about your goals and values, uncompromising about who you are, repellent to some so that you can be wildly attractive to others, and genuine about who you need to complete your mission, as that mission evolves you will become a beacon for the right employees. But still, even with all that effort, your team will continue to change. It is this change, this ebb and flow, that leaders must surrender to.

When I started my business, I thought building a team was about paying people to accomplish tasks. The truth is, it is very difficult to find humans who will accept money to complete tasks and do that effectively for very long. There is much more than a paycheck people are expecting from a job. Often, these days, that "much more" is called "work/life balance." This has become code for "I don't care how much they pay, I don't want to work that much." But really when you hear someone talking about work/life balance what they are talking about is a job where the expectations feel largely transactional. Work is not meant to be balanced with life.

Let's say we were balancing two things. A pile of pennies and a rock. Basically, what you have to do is figure out – by using a scale – how many pennies weigh the same as the rock. The pennies and the rock are 2 totally different items.

The penny is never a rock and the rock is never a penny.

The problem with the very idea of work/life balance is that work is a SUBSET of life. It's not a separate thing. You can't balance work on one side and life on the other – ever, because work is a part of your life, just like your health, your family, your hobbies, your chores, your bills are a part of your life. So, work/life balance is really just life balance and that scale has multiple measuring trays. You know when someone is saying they need a better work/life balance that there is more going on inside.

Work takes up too much time within your life to be something separate from it. In fact, I would argue that work is the BIGGEST single bucket of time within your life. So how could it be BALANCED against life, when it is such a big part of it?

There is no CONFLICT between work and life if your job is feeding your soul. If it is, you should look at the ways it is and amplify them. If it isn't, you should quit immediately.

Here's how work is a huge part of how I lead a balanced life.

Spiritual & Personal Growth – My job, where I spend 50-plus hours a week, is in the realm of spiritual and personal growth. Tactically I get to read books and interact with people on their theories about growth. In addition, I get to coach people on areas where I might be ahead of them. And MOST importantly, my job is SUPER HARD, and brings up LOTS AND LOTS of fear and resistance. Since I know the only way to address these is through my own spiritual and personal growth, work is one of the 3 best tools/mirrors in my life for creating growth (for me, the other 2 are my relationship and parenting; I know for others fitness or money is a great entry point to growth). Best of all, I work for a company that believes "Discomfort is Necessary for Growth" and encourages me to do uncomfortable things that stretch my limits and boundaries. If you don't feel this way about your job, it will be hard to have a balanced life, because for 40-60 hours a week you will be asked to ignore your spiritual and personal growth.

Romance – My job is amazing for romance. Many people meet their partners through work and with our incredible clients and staff I suppose this is possible. I love my job, so when I am with my partner I don't have to cut myself off from how I spend more than half of my waking hours. I'm proud of what I do and excited about it, so my job brings a lot of energy to my relationship. Also, sometimes we have sexy-time books I get early access to, which inspire me to explore that part of life in new ways.

Leisure – My job is amazing for leisure. Mostly because I meet people (coworkers and clients) from around the world who I get to go visit and even stay with for free. For me, travel and reading are my 2 favorite leisure activities. So yay! I read books I found through my job on the way to a long weekend with a coworker somewhere magical. Without my job, leisure would be a lot less fun. Oh! I also like spas and shopping as leisure activities and I've enjoyed both with team members and clients. How awesome is that!

Money – Well, duh, this one is obvious. There are other ways I could make money, but I choose my job as the way I make money right now and it's awesome. I'm paid fairly. There are lots of perks. If I were to look at all the ways I could make this much money or more, this is definitely the best-case scenario. Honestly, even if I had some trust fund, I am still pretty sure I'd be doing this job. The money is nice though. I mean, if you gotta pay your bills anyway, why do it in a job you hate?

Purpose – One of the things I love most about my job is that the people I work with value the idea of me being in my zone of genius. This means as much of the time as possible I am creating value for the company and our clients while living my purpose. So, the first thing for me in choosing this job was identifying my purpose. I didn't even know what my purpose was for a long time. I thought it was "to be happy" or "to make money" – totally wrong! When I stopped pegging my success against raises or promotions I realized happiness and money were BYPRODUCTS of living my purpose – and my purpose is to help others make a difference. I get to do that every day in my job. In fact, without my job, I guess I'd get some sense of purpose from trolling Facebook, but I'm not sure how I would incorporate purpose into my life. Oh, I know, I'd be doing more social justice theatre. That's what I did before this job. Protesting and activist theatre were my ways of making a difference.

Family – I've built a unique family and partnership and built them into the business. Yes, I'm the founder, so I can do that sort of thing, but there are ways your job can support your family – for instance, without this "work" I would not have the money to pay our rent or take vacations. Life wouldn't be MORE balanced if I didn't have this work because then there would be no money to take care of my family or enjoy my time with them.

Friends – Because we are so selective about who we work with – both clients and staff – I can say with 100% clarity that almost all of my friends are connected in some way to my work. I have a couple of old friends, but I consider my clients and co-workers – especially those who have been around since the early days – my closest friends. Because of that, this work has taught me to set exceptional boundaries with those friends who I work with, which has translated to closer relationships, even with non-work-related friends, because I'm such an amazing boundary-setter now.

Physical Environment – One of the awesome things about this work and why it supports balance in my life is that I have flexibility in terms of where I work, as do most of our employees. I LOVE coming in to the office – because... tacos, massages, world's best hugs, crystals – but when I need to let in the A/C guy it's no big deal to stay home. PLUS, the vibe in Georgetown, where our office is, is so fun I feel like I have so much more variety to my physical environment.

Health – Without work I would not be able to afford the health care coverage that I pay for and ignore while paying full price for all the health care I want which is mostly not covered.

I don't really understand insurance, but I think I'm grateful the company takes care of some of it. I am more grateful that our company culture supports and promotes self-care for real and that we are surrounded by sorcerers on the team who model self-care and inspire me to take better and better care of myself, because, yes, everything is a competition and I want to win the Best Self-Care Award!

Yes, I know this is easy for me to say because I'm the owner, but making this list is an exercise all of your employees should be able to do. They must understand how their job is supporting them to get all the things they want out of life, and it's your job to make sure their job is in alignment for them, or they will find a way to leave and blame you. But all of this is hard because you are human too.

You may miss the signs that a candidate is not a good fit, because you hit it off with them in the interview and went with that, or because the employee in charge of hiring really needed someone to fill the role. You will resist letting someone go because the timing feels bad for the business or in the employee's life.

I had a key employee who kicked ass in her role for 6 months and then near the holidays a switch flipped and she kept missing deadlines and just generally flaking out on everything. I blamed the holidays and decided to wait until January to reassess. January came and her mom was diagnosed with cancer. She was at the hospital more than the office and not getting work done, but I felt like the timing was off to let her go. Her mom passed and we had a serious "you have to turn things around here at work; I can't keep paying you to not work" conversation. She said she was committed to her job but the next month made it very clear that was not the case. Major milestones were dropped. Deadlines were missed. Her communication was sparse. It was clear the job was no longer in alignment for her but she didn't want to say it and neither did I.

Eventually I let her go, six months after I got the initial hit things were out of alignment. The problem was that not only was she not doing her job but her misaligned energy vortex sucked others in to it. Having a team member out of alignment has many hidden costs.

Even knowing what it takes to "make 'em beg to work for you," it's quite likely your tired and hopeful brain will want to bury your head in the sand. I have to caution you this will not work. You have to keep listening, keep improving, and know you are not going to be "done" – ever. Your business is an evolving superorganism that changes each day like the ocean. There is no "set it and forget it" button for a sports team and there isn't one for you either.

A lot of CEOs and even HR departments will try to paper over this fact with happy hours and costume parties. I can now understand where all the fake "rah-rah" corporate BS comes from. When I was an employee, I used to roll my eyes when they would hand out the free keychain with the company logo, or organize ice cream socials. It was bad enough when I had to stay late for work or to wait out traffic, but then I also had to stay late to kiss ass or make an appearance for some political reason. Forced fun is never fun to me. I am just not ever going to be that person.

The reason there is so much forced fun in the workplace is that we so desperately want employees to be happy. But the truth is, we can't make our employees happy. Most people are, in fact, not happy. I do think we can help our employees identify how this job is or isn't in alignment and encourage them to leave if it's not. I offer my team an annual window where I will give them a significant bonus if they quit because they have identified their job is not in alignment with what they really want in life.

In order for an employee to know if their job is in alignment, it's your job to be clear on who the organization is. You can be aligned with something squishy and unclear. So, the real problem at the end of the day is that most business owners are not willing to take a stand for who they are. When you look at the Virgin Group, which Richard Branson built, it's so clear who Virgin is and what it stands for. You can like it or not, but you can't be confused about it. When you think about AT&T, the answer isn't so clear. There is nothing to be aligned with because it's not clear who that brand is.

The purpose of branding is every bit as much for team-building as it is for client-getting.

I'm writing this chapter from the Great House on Richard Branson's Necker Island. It's 6 am. The rule on the island is you can work until lunchtime but then it's time for play. One of the event planners here is a lovely young woman from Newcastle in the UK named Camie. She has long legs, a Geordie accent and a big smile. I see her walking in to collect Katie, the community director for Virgin Unite, who is heading back to New York City today. I see them both as Virgin Group employees, sure, but each is on such a clear and different personal path.

Camie wants to see the world. She's lived and worked with her boyfriend Scott in Australia and now the two of them are here at Necker. Her personal goal is to be able to explore the world with her partner and without this job that wouldn't be possible. You can see in everything she does how grateful and in alignment this is. She arrived as a bartender 7 months ago and has already been promoted. She only goes home once a year and her parents think she's a little nuts, but Camie knows this is exactly where she is supposed to be.

Katie has been part of Virgin Unite for over 3 years as I write this, but her history of working for social justice is long. When you look at Katie's story, you see how she started biology and environmental conservation. The work she is able to do as part of Virgin Unite includes saving the oceans. But more than that, Katie started her own non-profit with three friends almost ten years ago to provide educational support to vulnerable children in Tanzania. Katie clearly has a mandate to solve social and ecological problems. She would be doing it on her own if she wasn't doing it here, as her resume makes clear. Her work doesn't need to be balanced with her life, because, like for Camie, this work is how she seeks expression in her life. They are not separate things. And Katie is probably going to make an even bigger impact with Richard Branson by her side then she would alone.

You don't have to have deep pockets like Richard Branson, but you do need to know who you are and where you are going so people like Camie and Katie will pursue working with you instead of you having to pursue them.

The prize never chases. Are you willing to do the work required to be the prize?

CHAPTER 12

The Multi-Orgasmic Business

Tom, one of the "water sports guys" at Necker Island is from Cornwall in England. Tom had a great job and a great life in Cornwall, but when a former employer told him about opportunities to teach Sir Richard kite-boarding and wind-foiling, he couldn't resist throwing his hat in the ring. It took weeks before he heard from the Necker team, and when he did he had 12 hours to make the decision about whether or not to take the job. There was a long line of people waiting to take his spot if he didn't want it. That is because the

Virgin Group is the kind of company people beg to work for.

Prospective candidates don't clamor to work for Virgin because of anything that could have been said or done in a single job interview or job posting; the work is much deeper and interconnected.

Throughout all aspects of society, systems are set up based on iterations of systems that were set up based on iterations of systems that were set up. True disruption happens, but it's rare and often at the surface. It can be hard to see what is really being disrupted.

The forerunner of the modern taxi cab was a horse-drawn for-hire hackney carriage service which began operating in the early 17th century. The carriages picked up passengers at hotels and, eventually, taxi stands in major cities like London and Paris. That seems like where the services were most needed or perhaps could best be afforded, but what it leaves out is the bulk of the population who never even knew those services existed. They were not distributed, but were contained and reserved for those with privilege. That system perpetuated and was iterated upon for 400 years with no one making a game-changing modification to the model until ride-sharing apps were introduced in 2009. Ride-sharing has a lower cost structure that makes rides available to many people who previously did not have access to many locations, including the young, elderly, and disabled. For drivers, the sharing services provide an alternative to driving themselves, especially when drinking. For some people, especially women facing assault and danger, being able to call a car has increased safety – and it has reduced arrest rates for assault and disorderly conduct.

I'm not saying the ride-sharing model is without problems. It's clear there are as many problems with this more distributed, less managed approach to getting a ride from a stranger; but put aside the pros and cons argument and just look at the structure itself. It's gone from simple, single-pointed, and all or nothing – to more complicated, multi-faceted, and much greyer. This is how everything is trending in society.

We are moving from a masculine model of everything, which is competitive, assertive, goal-driven, pushing forward, and singular, to a feminine model of everything, which is nurturing, relationship-oriented, interdependent, multi-tasking, and collaborative.

This is happening with team-building too. We used to think of creating teams as happening at a fixed point in time – you go out there and "get" the stars (sort of like the raping of the Sabine women) and then you "have" them do your bidding. Ah, the good old days when the voices of the masses were successfully suppressed.

Thank the millennials for figuring this one out for us. If you are going to build a great team now, you are going to need to build something collaborative, intuitive, and harmonious to attract top talent. And that talent is only going to beg to work for you if they know the relationship you will have is give and take, not one-sided.

In short, we have moved from the transactional days of "just lie back and think of England" to a multi-orgasmic future when we are all on a lesbian commune sharing the workload on all levels.

This isn't about right and wrong, or even male and female – it's about the way society is shifting toward a more complicated and interconnected multi-tasking world where there is no big, single WIN (think male orgasm here for the visual), but instead there are lots of different and delightful feminine explosions.

There's No I in COMPANY

A modern business that embraces the feminine leadership qualities required for the information age is a COMPANY, just like a theatre troupe is a COMPANY of actors. If you want your COMPANY to be blessed with amazing talent begging to work for you, here are the 7 steps I taught in this book.

Step 1: Culture First

A company worthy of having prospective employees beating down its doors to work for them has a clear vision of who they are, where they are going, and what they want the team to look like. In this book I have given recommendations about doing that with an eye to diversity, because without thinking about creating safe spaces for all people you will not be able to get the best candidates to build your dream.

Step 2: Operate in the Future

I recommended starting with an organizational chart so you can really understand the total workload. Most people hire in a way that creates problems instead of solving them because they don't really have a handle on how to narrow responsibilities to create true accountability.

Step 3: Market to Your Prospective Workers

Based on my experience with direct response marketing, I recommend writing the job description as a sales letter to the person who is most ideal for the position. Make sure you understand the dream come true of your perfect candidate before you write the post!

Step 4: Pick the winners

Before you get to the interview, use a project to make sure the person is capable of the tasks, but know most success comes from alignment. During the interview, your role is to assess whether the connection will serve the highest and best for all and if the job is in true alignment with candidate's life purpose. Pro-tip: When prospects are totally unclear on what they want or what their next goal is, they are going to be unsure and unstable in the role. Can you imagine agreeing to marry someone who wasn't sure if they wanted to be married? That's the equivalent. It doesn't work. You can make them a freelance contractor though.

Once you have a candidate you are ready to make an offer to, be like the Virgin Group and give a very short window for decision-making. Ideally, they will decide on the spot – 24 hours is the longest I recommend. Ask yourself if they would they need that long if Beyoncé or Sir Richard were offering the job?

Step 5: Align the compensation

Remember, compensation and raises are pieces of the puzzle –important pieces – but not nearly as important as you think. People want to be treated with respect and have the opportunity to make a real impact. They need to get their bills paid, sure, but compensation is not the ultimate decider. And bonuses have been shown to decrease productivity.

Excellence comes from having intrinsic motivation. Dan Pink describes three types of intrinsic motivation: "Autonomy – The urge to direct our own lives. Mastery – The desire to get better and better at something that matters. Purpose – The yearning to do what we do in the service of something larger than ourselves."

We saw with Richard Branson's employees Camie and Katie how their jobs tied to their intrinsic motivation. On the other hand, Dr. Bernd Irlenbusch of the London School of Economics found that financial incentives "can result in a negative impact on overall performance."

Giving out bonuses is a cheap trick that simply doesn't work in the more divinely feminine business structures that are emerging.

Step 6: Nurture your Talent

Sink or swim is an expensive and entitled approach. Getting great team members is too hard and requires too much effort to drop them at the first mistake. Communication is difficult, impossible maybe. And the old hire slow, fire fast approach is not a fit for this labor market or the world of social media and online reviews. Protect your investment and nurture your talent.

Step 7: Yield with Love

Finally, when it comes to onboarding and off-boarding employees to create an institution people will make sacrifices to work for, the key is to go slow, nurture the relationship, trust your intuition, and guide and support your employee in trusting their intuition. The answers are not outside, so finding those answers is an inside job. Trust and patience are the new required skills.

I'll leave you with one final thought about how business is becoming feminine: To attract the top talent you have to lean into your divine feminine too – no matter what your gender is.

In 2012, as part of the New York Times best-selling book The Athena Doctrine, there was survey done of 64,000 people around the world asking them about the characteristics of the "ideal modern leader." Of the top ten competencies expressed, only 2 (decisiveness and resiliency) were viewed as masculine. The other 8 – expressiveness, visionary, reasonable, loyal, flexible, patient, intuitive, and collaborative – were viewed as feminine.

The future is indeed female. And to "make 'em beg to work for you," you will need to create feminine structures in your business, unless all your employees are going to be 45 and aging.

Millennials are the majority of the workforce now and they have lit the way. The bar is high, but my wish for you is a kick-ass team of 2 or 20,000 people who wouldn't dream of working anywhere else than by your side, making your visions real.

Be the change.

ACKNOWLEDGMENTS

This book would not have happened if it weren't for The Collective, a group of 6-, 7-, and 8-figure-earning female CEOs who are committed to world peace, social justice, civil rights, healing the environment, making money, having fun, and eating well while doing all of it.

The book was conceived during a trip The Collective took to Sir Richard Branson's private game reserve in South Africa called Ulusaba, then completed on his private island resort, Necker, in the British Virgin Islands. While I was in Ulusaba, I asked Richard why he wrote his books and he said, "If you can make a difference, you gotta get out there and make a difference. I think you have a responsibility in life to write a book."

I'd written books before he said that, of course, but always books to benefit me and my business. This book is different. I wrote this one for my sisters – women building empires and trying to figure out how to get a kick-ass team behind them for the journey. I didn't HAVE TO write this book, but I felt like it was my responsibility to share my difficult and unlikely journey of falling in love with team-building.

In addition to Sir Richard Branson himself and Katie Hunt-Morr on his Virgin Unite team, I'd specifically I'd like to thank the leader of The Collective, Natalie MacNeil. I also want to thank my Collective sisters. First, thanks to the OG crew – Alex Beadon, Denise Duffield-Thomas, Moriah Coz, Jennifer Kem, Amanda Bond, Diana House, Amanda Daley, and Adrienne Dorison. What a ride! I have loved watching your massive uplevels through the years. I am grateful for all I've learned from you. And from all the other members too, but especially Susan Hyatt, one of my first #incubatedauthors – sharing this empire-building adventure with you has been a great joy of mine and a true testament to the #togetherwerise philosophy that drives me forward even when it feels too hard to go on. Thanks to my South African travel buddies,

Chantelle Brunisma, Maggie Berghoff, Birgit Esselmont, Layla Martin, Jennifer Evans, Kate McKibbin, Niyc Pidgeon, Ange Loughran. And thanks to the women who joined us in Necker, Neha Gupta (my sister from another mister), Jen Gottlieb (my guardian angel), Elizabeth Purvis, Jade Jemma, Paige Filliater, Melyssa Griffin, Erin Brule, Lisa DiGeso, Abbey Askley, Carrie Green, and the beautiful Ruth Soukup. Plus, all the spouses, kids and other plus-ones who delighted us with their presence.

I also want to thank the woman who inspired this book's creation with her presence in my life, Rae Guyn. I hired Rae a few years ago, before I realized the transactional model of leadership was not going to work. It was her sheer excellence in every way that inspired me to be a better leader. I didn't know how to do it for me, but I was willing to figure it out for her. I knew from her first few months that she had what it took to be the second CEO of The Author Incubator. It was a weird knowing. And the message it came with was loud and clear – to make that happen, I had to step up and be a much better leader. I have tried to honor that calling and I see her every day as my greatest teacher in business management. Thanks for being so brave and vulnerable, smart and committed, and willing and wonderful. You inspire me!

I feel like all my employees are my soulmates, but some soulmate employees have hard lessons to teach, like Kara Ghassabeh. During the writing of this book, Kara quit. She quit in one of those "take this job and shove it" ways I was writing about just as she was quitting. It was clear it could not be a coincidence. She was also an angel, here to teach me a difficult and painful lesson. Kara quit because I lost her trust. And I lost her trust because I didn't present feedback to her in a very professional manner. Understandably, she decided she wasn't going to work in a place where she was treated like that.

I attempted to apologize and she replied by saying it wasn't a big deal. But it is.

My behavior called for an apology to Kara and also to the entire team, and I provided one. I told them that my inability to act professionally caused us to lose an awesome team member and I am deeply heartbroken and apologetic.

It was a reminder that all my suggestions I've shared in this book are easier said than done. I forgot my own system because I was scared. I let myself down and I let the team down and I shared that with everyone. It's no secret that I don't always get these steps right. But I do always try, because I know for sure I cannot build this company without having an aligned team of fellow magic-makers building this dream alongside me.

In addition to thanking Rae and Kara, I want to give thanks to the entire team at The Author Incubator. It has been my honor to have earned your trust, and I promise to continue to do my best to deserve it.

To my editor Grace Kerina who has been in this COMPANY in so many ways at this point it's hard to count. She was one of the first people on my team and many of the stories in the book were ones she experienced first-hand. I have not always been so clear on the role of management and team building but I learned a lot about it from Grace and for that, and her expert editing in this book, I am humbled and grateful.

Two other special team shout-outs – first to Robin Thompson, who has been building this business with me almost since the beginning. I know from the tips of my toes that God brought us together. I am constantly surprised we were assigned to fulfill this mission together, but working with you always feels like coming home. I'm so grateful for all the ways we communicate, but especially the ones that don't require words.

And thanks to my director of finance, my savior, and my ex-husband, who I love now even more than when we were married, Paul Brycock. We have had so many miracles in our relationship. This year has been another one and I know there are more to come. I am so grateful we made it through in our own wacky and weird way. Thanks for being such an amazing part of the team and my life.

Love always to The Rocknroll Family. It's ironic we picked that name after hearing about it from Richard Branson's nephew just after the big fire on Necker. How prophetic – we really are kind of part of Richard's family, right? He just doesn't totally know it yet.

To Mila, my parenting partner and chief of staff at The Author Incubator and our 3 gorgeous kids – Sofia, Lauti, and my Jesse. I love you guys and I'm so grateful you love me too.

Finally, I'd like to acknowledge the incredible hospitality of the staff on Necker Island, where this book was written. Special thanks to Kamie, Jess, Beth, Indian, Jamdown, Jovan, and Scott for taking extra special good care of me while I was writing!

.

ABOUT THE AUTHOR

Dr. Angela E. Lauria is the founder of The Author Incubator™ and creator of the Difference Process™ for writing a book that matters. In 2018, The Author Incubator was ranked #275 on the Inc. 500 list of fastest-growing companies, and #87 on Entrepreneur Magazine's Entrepreneur 360. Dr. Angela won the Stevie Award's Coach/Mentor of the Year Award. Her program, The Author's Way, was named Coaching Program of the Year. She was named by Entrepreneur Magazine as one of the top 10 most inspiring entrepreneurs to watch – one of only 2 women on the list.

Dr. Angela has been helping people free their inner authors since 1994 and has helped over 1,000 authors-in-transformation write, publish, and promote their books. Her clients have been seen everywhere, from Vanity Fair to O Magazine to the Today show, and their books have been responsible for over $100 million in cumulative revenue.

She has a BA and an MA in Journalism and Media Affairs from The George Washington University and a PhD in Communications from The European Graduate School. She is the author of *Make 'Em Beg to Be Your Client: The Nonfiction Authors' Guide to Selling, Serving, and Funding a Movement*, *Make 'Em Beg to Publish Your Book: How to Reach a Larger Audience & Make a Full-Time Income in The Extremely Overcrowded World of Personal Development*, *The Incubated Author: 10*

Steps to Start a Movement with Your Message, and The Difference: 10 Steps to Writing a Book That Matters. She lives at The Author Castle in McLean, Virginia, with her son Jesse and her Castle cats – Princesses Feathers and Foxy McFuzz Bucket.

ABOUT DIFFERENCE PRESS

Difference Press is the exclusive publishing arm of The Author Incubator, an educational company for entrepreneurs, including life coaches, healers, consultants, and community leaders, looking for a comprehensive solution to get their books written, published, and promoted. Its founder, Dr. Angela Lauria, has been bringing to life the literary ventures of hundreds of authors-in-transformation since 1994.

A boutique-style self-publishing service for clients of The Author Incubator, Difference Press boasts a fair and easy-to-understand profit structure, low-priced author copies, and author-friendly contract terms. Most importantly, all of our #incubatedauthors maintain ownership of their copyright at all times.

Let's Start a Movement with Your Message

In a market where hundreds of thousands of books are published every year and are never heard from again, The Author Incubator is different. Not only do all Difference Press books reach Amazon bestseller status, but all of our authors are actively changing lives and making a difference.

Since launching in 2013, we've served over 500 authors who came to us with an idea for a book and were able to write it and get it self-published in less than 6 months. In addition, more than 100 of those books were picked up by traditional publishers and are now available in book stores. We do this by selecting the highest quality and highest potential applicants for our future programs.

Our program doesn't just teach you how to write a book – our team of coaches, developmental editors, copy editors, art directors, and marketing experts incubate you from book idea to published bestseller, ensuring that the book you create can actually make a difference in the world. Then we give you the training you need to use your book to make the difference in the world, or to create a business out of serving your readers.

Are You Ready to Make a Difference?

You've seen other people make a difference with a book. Now it's your turn. If you are ready to stop watching and start taking massive action, go to http://theauthorincubator.com/apply/.

"Yes, I'm ready!"

OTHER BOOKS BY DR. ANGELA LAURIA

The Difference: 10 Steps to Writing a Book that Matters (Released December 13, 2014)

The Incubated Author: 10 Steps to Start a Movement with Your Message (Released January 17, 2016)

Make 'Em Beg to Publish Your Book: How to Reach a Larger Audience & Make a Full-Time Income in the Extremely Overcrowded World of Personal Development (Released May 15, 2017)

Make 'Em Beg to Be Your Client: The Nonfiction Authors' Guide to Selling, Serving, and Funding a Movement (Released March 21, 2018)

OTHER BOOKS BY DIFFERENCE PRESS

Career Defense 101: Is Your Career Safe from Sexism? by Meredith Holley

...But I'm Not Racist!: Tools for Well-Meaning Whites by Kathy Obear

Twice as Good: Leadership and Power for Women of Color by Mary J. Wardell

The Relationship Roadmap: The Spiritual Guidebook to Ditch the Uncertainty and Find Clarity in Your Marriage by Kelli Reese

HELP! My Kid Wants to Become a YouTuber: Your Child Can Learn Life Skills While Having a TON OF FUN Creating Online Videos by Michael Buckley and Jesse Malhotra

If you have life-or world-changing ideas or services, a servant's heart, and the willingness to do what it REALLY takes to make a difference in the world with your book, go to **http://theauthorincubator.com/apply/** to complete an application for the program today.

THANKS FOR READING

If you really follow the whole Make' Em Beg to Work for You formula, you will realize what's special about the job descriptions you write is very different than what's special about the ones I write. You have to be you. Your descriptions have to make people feel what it will be like to work at your organization.

However, I know people love reading our job descriptions – almost like eating dessert! Plus, it might give you some good ideas and creative license to be even more yourself in your posts. I've put all my job descriptions into a single document that you can download totally free at **www.TheAuthorIncubator.com/JDs**.

You can also follow us in social media and learn more about us and our Rockstar team.

Facebook – The Author Incubator
Instagram – @AuthorIncubator
Linked In –linkedin.com/company/1589902
Twitter – @AuthorIncubator

www.ingramcontent.com/pod-product-compliance
Lightning Source LLC
Chambersburg PA
CBHW060829220526
45466CB00003B/1029